Nelson English

Pupil Book 4

Wendy Wren and Sarah Lindsay

OXFORD
UNIVERSITY PRESS

OXFORD
UNIVERSITY PRESS

Great Clarendon Street, Oxford, OX2 6DP, United Kingdom

Oxford University Press is a department of the University of Oxford. It furthers the University's objective of excellence in research, scholarship, and education by publishing worldwide. Oxford is a registered trade mark of Oxford University Press in the UK and in certain other countries.

Text © Wendy Wren and Sarah Lindsay 2018
The moral rights of the author have been asserted.

First published 2018

British Library Cataloguing in Publication Data

Data available

ISBN: 978-0-1984-1982-2

5 7 9 10 8 6

Paper used in the production of this book is a natural, recyclable product made from wood grown in sustainable forests. The manufacturing process conforms to the environmental regulations of the country of origin.

Printed in China by Golden Cup

Acknowledgements
Series consultant: John Jackman

Cover and inside illustrations by Q2A Media Services Inc.

Page make-up by Aptara

The publisher and authors would like to thank the following for permission to use photographs and other copyright material:

p24: imageBROKER/Alamy Stock Photo; **p48(b, tl):** Dreamstime; **p60(tl), 62(tl):** ChristinLola/iStockphoto; **p60(br):** © Getty Images; **p84(b):** MarkMalkinsonPhotography/iStockphoto; **p86:** Universal Images Group North America LLC/Alamy Stock Photo; **p88:** John Downer/Nature Picture Library. All other photos © Shutterstock.

Every effort has been made to acknowledge copyright holders of material reproduced in this book. Any omissions will be rectified in subsequent printings if notice is given to the publisher.

We are grateful for permission to reproduce the following copyright material:

Madhur Jaffrey: extract from 'The Mango Tree' from *Seasons of Splendour* (Pavilion 1985), copyright © Madhur Jaffrey 1985, reproduced by permission of the author c/o Rogers, Coleridge & White Ltd, 20 Powis Mews, London W11 1JN.

Terry Jones: extract from *The Saga of Erik the Viking* (Pavilion, 2016), copyright © Terry Jones 1983, reproduced by permission of Pavilion Books Company Ltd.

Clive King: extract from *Stig of the Dump* (Viking Kestrel, 1980), copyright © Clive King 1963, reproduced by permission of David Higham Associates.

Marilyn Lott: 'My Rainbow Garden', copyright © Marilyn Lott, published on poemhunter.com, reproduced by permission of the author.

Naomi Lewis: extract from 'The Snow Queen' from *Hans Christian Andersen's Fairy Tales* chosen and translated by Naomi Lewis (Puffin, 1995), translation copyright © Naomi Lewis 1981, reproduced by permission of Penguin Books Ltd.

Iain Crichton Smith: 'The Rainbow', copyright © Iain Crichton Smith 1983 from *New Collected Poems* edited by Matt McGuire (Carcanet, 2011), reproduced by permission of the author's Estate and Carcanet Press Ltd.

Although we have made every effort to trace and contact all copyright holders before publication this has not been possible in all cases. If notified, the publisher will rectify any errors or omissions at the earliest opportunity.

Contents

Book 4 Scope and Sequence

Unit	Unit Title	Text	Comprehension Focus	Vocabulary Focus
1	Who Were the Vikings?	Information text: 'The Vikings'	Investigating paragraphs in non-fiction	Word ending and suffixes
2	Erik the Viking	Fiction text: extract from *The Saga of Erik the Viking* by Terry Jones	Analysing plot	Rhyming wor
3	A Chinese Play	Short play script: 'The Painter and the Judge'	Investigating scenes in play scripts	Alphabetical order
4	The Great Wall of China	Magazine article: 'A Must-See!' Fact file: 'The Great Wall of China'	Analysing purpose	Alphabetical order
5	Castles in Stories	Fiction texts: extracts from *The Fisherman's Castle* by the Brothers Grimm and *The Snow Queen's Castle* by Hans Christian Andersen	Imagining yourself in the story	Gender word
6	Let's Celebrate!	Information text: 'New Year Celebrations' Instructions: 'The Firework Code'	Investigating instructional writing	Words used as nouns and verbs
7	Stig of the Dump	Fiction text: extract from *Stig of the Dump* by Clive King	Analysing the setting and characters in a story	Synonyms an phrases
8	Reduce, Reuse, Recycle	Information text: 'Dealing with Waste'	Analysing information texts	Over-used word: nice
9	Rainbow Poems	Poetry: 'The Rainbow' by Iain Crichton Smith and 'My Rainbow Garden' by Marilyn Lott	Analysing description and rhyme schemes in poetry	Using a dictionary
10	Books About Bridges	Extracts from three non-fiction texts about bridges	Identifying key words and phrases	Definitions
11	Robert Louis Stevenson	Biographical text: 'Robert Louis Stevenson: A Biography'	Analysing a biographical text	Antonyms
12	Treasure Island	Fiction text: extract adapted from *Treasure Island* by Robert Louis Stevenson	Reading and responding to first person narratives	Using a thesaurus
13	Wildfire	Fiction text: extract from *Wildfire* by Mavis Thorpe Clark	Looking at how writers add detail to narrative writing	Synonyms fo 'said'
14	Fire Beneath Our Feet	Explanatory text: 'Volcanoes'	Investigating explanatory writing	Synonyms
15	The Mango Tree	Fiction text: extract from *The Mango Tree* by Madhur Jaffrey	Exploring a resolution to a character's problems	Diminutives
16	Travelling in India	Advertisement: 'India will amaze you!'	Analysing a persuasive text	Similes
17	On Top of the World	Newspaper report: 'First Sri Lankan Climber to Reach Everest Summit!'	Analysing a newspaper article	Homophones

Punctuation Focus	Spelling Focus	Grammar Focus	Writing Focus
Punctuating sentences	**ur** and **ure** word endings	Paragraphing in non-fiction writing	Factual writing
Direct speech	Syllables	Verb round-up	Planning a story
Dialogue in plays	**ive** word ending	Noun round-up	Play scripts
Commas in lists	**ea** words	The present perfect tense	Factual writing
Singular possessive nouns	**f/fe** word endings	Adjectives	Settings for stories
Using bullet points	Suffixes **ship** and **hood**	The present perfect tense: regular and irregular verbs	Instructions
Apostrophes of contraction	**en** and **on** word endings	Noun phrases	Setting and characters
Plural possessive nouns	Prefixes **un**, **mis**, **dis** and **re**	Singular and plural	Information texts
Apostrophes of contraction	Silent letters	Possessive adjectives and possessive pronouns	Poetry
Commas in numbers	**sion**, **ssion** and **cian** word endings	Past perfect tense	Collecting information
Plural and possessive nouns	The prefixes **auto**, **super** and **anti**	Pronouns and possessive adjectives	Biographical writing
Direct speech – speaker's name first	Prefixes **in**, **im**, **il** and **ir**	Paragraphing in fiction	First person narrative
Direct speech – questions and exclamations	**ly** word ending	Noun and verb agreement	Story endings
it's or its?	**tion** word ending	Adverb clauses	Summaries
Split direct speech	**able** and **ible** suffixes	Verb tense round-up	Solving problems
Commas in lists	**ous**, **ious** and **eous** word endings	Fronted adverb clauses	Advertisements
Indirect speech	Words from French	Fronted adverb clauses	Newspaper reports

Who Were the Vikings?

The Vikings

The Vikings came from an area in northern Europe called Scandinavia. This area is made up of Norway, Sweden and Denmark. They lived between 700 CE and 1100 CE. They made their living from **agriculture**, fishing and trading, and they were fierce fighters!

The lands where the Vikings lived were mountainous and covered in forests. This meant making a living from farming was very difficult. Much of their food came from fishing along the Scandinavian coast. Many of the Vikings looked for an easier life in other lands.

The Vikings were expert boat builders. They built large open rowing boats that were pointed at each end. The boats were narrow and very long. This made them fast and easy to row. There was usually a **crew** of 60, taking it in turns to row at 30 oars. These longboats were used for raiding and plundering along the coast of other countries.

Glossary

agriculture farming
crew the people who work together on a ship
cargo goods carried on a ship
archaeologists people who dig in the ground to find historical remains
settlements places where people make their homes

A Viking longboat

Boats for trading were wider and had higher sides than longboats. Each boat could carry four or five tonnes of **cargo** such as furs, and travel thousands of kilometres.

Vikings travelled far across the seas to trade and settle. **Archaeologists** have found the remains of Viking **settlements** in Britain, southern Europe, Iceland, Greenland and even as far as North America. No one is sure how they managed to travel such great distances as they had no charts or compasses to guide them.

Some Vikings returned to their homeland but others settled where they landed, farming and fishing to make a living. Their families and their animals often joined them in their new land.

Word Check

You can use a dictionary to help you.

A Find each word in the extract. Choose the correct meaning.

1 mountainous   **a** covered in mountains
                          b flat

2 expert   **a** not very good at
                      b very good at

3 plundering   **a** fishing
                        b stealing

4 remains   **a** all of something
                        b what is left of something

B Find these phrases in the extract. Discuss what they mean.

1 made their living   2 used for raiding

Comprehension

A Discuss the answers to these questions.

1 Where did the Vikings come from?

2 What countries make up Scandinavia?

3 How did the Vikings 'make their living'?

4 What were the Vikings 'expert' at doing?

B Write a sentence to answer each question.

1 Explain in your own words why 'making a living from farming was very difficult'.

2 Why do you think the longboats were 'pointed at each end'?

3 Why do you think it is surprising that the Vikings could travel 'far across the seas'?

4 How do we know that the Vikings sailed as far as North America?

C Make **brief notes** on what each **paragraph** in the extract is about.

Vocabulary

Word endings and suffixes

> Remember, a **suffix** is a word ending.

The words in the following pairs are similar because they are from the same word family, but they have different endings, or **suffixes**.

inva**sion**	inv**ade**
terr**ible**	terr**ify**
crea**tion**	cre**ate**

A Add **ify** or **ate** to each group of letters to make a word.

1 horr_____   2 educ_____   3 oper_____

4 ident_____   5 irrit_____   6 simpl_____

B For each word below, make a new word from the same word family that ends with **ion**.

The first one has been done to help you.

1 navigate   <u>navigation</u>

2 cultivate   3 calculate   4 accelerate

5 situate   6 evaporate   7 congratulate

8 agitate   9 anticipate   10 regulate

C Choose three of the **ion** words that you made in **Activity B** and use each one in a sentence of your own.

Punctuation

Punctuating sentences

> All **sentences** begin with a **capital letter**. A **statement** ends with a **full stop**. For example:
>
>   The Vikings came from Scandinavia.
>
> A **question** ends with a **question mark**. For example:
>
>   Who were the Vikings?
>
> An **exclamation** ends with an **exclamation mark**. For example:
>
>   The Vikings were fierce fighters!

A Copy the sentences. End each one with a **full stop** or a **question mark** or an **exclamation mark**.

1 Do you know where the Vikings came from

2 The Vikings were very good at building boats

3 Viking longboats were amazing

4 They were such fierce fighters

5 Would you like to be a Viking

6 Some Vikings settled where they landed

Spelling

ur and **ure** word endings

> The **ure** spelling pattern is often found with the **sure** and **ture** suffixes.

> The **ur** spelling pattern occurs quite often.
>   Each boat could carry four or five tonnes
>   of cargo such as f**ur**s ...
>   They made their living from agricult**ure**, fishing and trading.

A Find the **ur** or **ure** word in the box that matches each picture.

nurse	puncture	treasure	picture	purse	burn

1

2

3

4

5

6

10

B Write each of the words in **Activity A** in your own sentences.

> Sometimes there can be two **ur sounds** in a word and the sounds can be made from **different letter patterns**.
> fi**r**m**er**

C Copy these words and underline the **ur** sounds in each one.

1 burner

2 learner

3 surgery

4 dirtier

Grammar

Paragraphing in non-fiction writing

> A **paragraph** is a group of sentences about **one main idea**.

Having **paragraphs** in **non-fiction writing** makes it easier for readers to follow.

We begin a **new paragraph** when we write about a **different aspect** of a topic. We show a new paragraph has started by starting a new line.

In *The Vikings*, there are **six paragraphs**. The writer has written about **six different aspects** of the topic.

paragraph 1: where the Vikings came from

paragraph 2: difficulty of life at home

paragraph 3: longboats

paragraph 4: trading boats

paragraph 5: how far they travelled

paragraph 6: settling in new lands

A Here is some more information about the Vikings. The information is in the form of **notes**. Read the notes carefully.

1 Vikings – settled in Britain – brought their families

2 houses – wooden walls – thatched roofs – fire in the centre – fences all around

3 Viking shops – weavers made cloth – jewellers sold rings and beads – Vikings made things from wood for example bowls, metal for example coins.

B Use the notes in **Activity A** to write **three paragraphs** about the Vikings.

Writing

Factual writing

Factual writing is **true** and gives the reader **information**.
The Vikings is a factual text giving information about:

- when the Vikings lived
- where they came from
- how they made their living
- what they were good at
- how far they travelled
- where they settled.

The Vikings is written in **paragraphs** to make it easier for readers to follow.

1 You are going to write some factual information about yourself. You will need to make **notes** about:

- your name, age and what you look like
  - the colour of your hair and eyes
  - how tall you are
- the members of your family
  - how many brothers and sisters you have
  - their names
  - if you are an only child
  - if other family members such as grandparents, aunts and uncles live with you
- what you like/dislike doing in school and why
- your hobbies
  - things you like doing by yourself
  - things you like doing with others

2 Use your notes to write **four factual paragraphs** about yourself.

UNIT 2 Erik the Viking

This is the beginning of a tale of a Viking warrior who lived hundreds and hundreds of years ago. His name was Erik. His ship was called *Golden Dragon*, and its figurehead was a fierce monster carved out of wood and covered in gold leaf.

One day, Erik said to his wife, "I must find the land where the sun goes at night." But his wife replied, "No one has ever been to that far country. And of those who have tried few have ever returned."

"You are right," said Erik, "but, until I have sought that distant land, I shall never sleep in my bed again."

So he called his son who was fifteen years old and told him he must guard their home by day and night. Then he took his sword, which was called *Blueblade*, stepped on board *Golden Dragon* and sailed off towards the setting sun.

That night they sailed on far from land, and Erik stood at the **helm** of *Golden Dragon*, gazing into the darkness. Erik's men whispered to each other that they were seeking the land where the sun goes at night, and that no one had ever found it and lived to tell the tale.

The next morning they found themselves alone on the ocean with great waves heaving the ship up and down. Erik looked up into the sky and smelt the wind.

"We shan't make it!" whispered Erik's men, one to the other, as the storm clouds blotted out the sun.

"We'll be wrecked at sea," they murmured as the first drops of rain fell on the deck.

"There's land!" called Erik. "Take down the sails … we'll have to row for it."

They leant on their oars as the rain began to pour down on them. And the speck of land on the horizon got bigger as the skies got darker and the sea grew rougher.

Glossary

helm where the ship is steered from

port the left side of a ship when facing forward

starboard the right side of a ship when facing forward

fjord a sheltered section of the sea between high rocks

But they rowed with all their might and main, and, as the lightening forked across the heavens and the thunder rolled all around them, they got closer and closer to land.

"Rocks to **port**!" cried the look out, and *Golden Dragon* swung round to **starboard**. "Rocks to starboard!" cried the look out, and *Golden Dragon* swung back to port again.

"Look out ahead!" cried Erik, and the golden monster on the helm scraped against the rocks as the sea dragged them down and then threw them up again.

"We've had it now!" cried Erik's men one to the other and they shut their eyes.

"Keep rowing!" cried Erik, and he steered the ship between the rocks and the boiling sea until, all at once, they found themselves in a deep **fjord**. One by one Erik's men opened their eyes. The rain still poured down on them and the lightning lit up the wild rocks above them, but the water was calm and they were safe.

The Saga of Erik the Viking by Terry Jones

Word Check

You can use a dictionary to help you.

A Find each word or phrase in the story. Choose the correct meaning.

1 sought   **a** looked for
                     b seen

2 heaving   **a** turning
                     b lifting

3 blotted out   **a** surrounded
                     b covered

4 wrecked   **a** destroyed
                     b saved

B Find these phrases and sentences in the story. Discuss what they mean.

1 lived to tell the tale   2 We shan't make it!

3 with all their might and main   4 We've had it now!

Comprehension

A Discuss the answers to these questions.

1 What was the name of Erik's longboat?

2 What was Erik determined to do?

3 How old was Erik's son?

4 What was the weather like when *Golden Dragon* was at sea?

5 While Erik steered the ship, what did he order his men to do?

B Write a sentence to answer each question.

1 Where on the longboat would you find the 'figurehead'?

2 How do you think Erik's wife felt about the journey?

3 How do you think Erik's son felt about guarding their home?

4 Why do you think Erik's men 'shut their eyes'?

5 How do you think Erik's men were feeling during the storm?

C Using words and phrases from the extract, make brief notes about the stages in the plot:

1 how Erik is introduced

2 how we find out about the journey

3 the beginning of the storm

4 how Erik and his men react

5 how Erik gets them to safety

Rhyming words

Making up your own rhymes is fun. **Limericks** are short and funny rhymes that have five lines.

Can you see which lines rhyme with each other in this limerick?

> There was an old Viking I kn**ew**
> Who loved to eat cabbage and st**ew**.
> So when they ran **out**
> He gave a great sh**out**
> And cried, "Now, what else can I ch**ew**?"

A Make a list of all the words you can think of that rhyme with each word below.

The first one is done for you.

1 sheep <u>deep, jeep, keep, weep,</u>
          <u>sleep, creep, heap, leap</u>

Notice that **sheep** and **heap** rhyme, even though they have different letter patterns.

2 zoom   3 cake

4 mice   5 bean

B Choose one of the sets of rhyming words that you made in **Activity A**. Use the words to help you write a limerick or other rhyme.

Direct speech

Direct speech is when we write the actual words someone has spoken.

We use **speech marks** at the **beginning** and **end** of the spoken words.

We can use a **comma** to separate the spoken and non-spoken words.

"I must find the land where the sun goes at night," said Erik.

We can also use a **question mark** or an **exclamation mark** at the end of the spoken words.

The punctuation after the spoken words always comes **before** the speech marks.

"Where is father going?" asked his son.

"Rocks to port!" cried the look out.

A Copy the sentences. Add the missing **speech marks**.

The first one is done for you.

1 Where are we going? asked the sailors.
  <u>"Where are we going?" asked the sailors.</u>

2 I want to go with you, said Erik's son.

3 Please be careful! said Erik's wife.

4 You must keep rowing! ordered Erik.

5 We are safe now, Erik said.

B Write two direct speech sentences using speech marks and:

   1 a **question mark**

   2 an **exclamation mark**

Spelling

Syllables

> In some short words, the letter **y** acts as a vowel, and makes a vowel sound.

> **Syllables** are the sounds that make up a word. Each syllable makes a sound of its own.
>
> All syllables contain a **vowel** or a **vowel sound**.
>
>   **tale** is pronounced as **one sound**, so it has **one syllable**
>
>   **darkness** is pronounced **dark-ness**, so it has **two syllables**
>
>   **horizon** is pronounced **hor-i-zon**, so it has **three syllables**.

A Draw a table like the one below.

Look at the extract from *Erik the Viking* on **pages 14 and 15**. Find and write down six words under each column.

One-syllable words	Two-syllable words	Three-syllable words

B Write a word that rhymes with each of the following words and has the same number of syllables.

   1 tunnel   <u>funnel</u>

   2 town   **3** spoiling

   4 muddle   **5** trying

   6 breaking   **7** mood

   8 clattering **9** goat

> The first one is done for you.

Verb round-up

Remember, **verbs** are action or doing words. The **tense** of a verb tells us **when** the action happens.

- If the action happens in the **present**, we use a **present tense**.

  present simple   **present progressive**
  Erik **sails** his ship.   OR   Erik **is sailing** his ship.

- If the action happens in the **past**, we use a **past tense**.

  past simple   **past progressive**
  Erik **called** his son.   OR   They **were rowing**.

  Some **past simple** verbs are irregular.

  He **took** his sword.   *Golden Dragon* **swung** round.

- If the action happens in the **future**, we use the **future tense**.

  future with will   **future with shall**
  Erik **will steer** them.   We **shall row** for that land!

A Copy the sentences and underline the verbs.

1 Erik called his son.   2 He looked at the sky.

3 They took the sails down.   4 They leant on their oars.

5 The sea dragged them down.   6 The men closed their eyes.

B Match the **present simple** verbs in **Box A** with the **past simple** verbs in **Box B**. Write the pairs of verbs.

Box A		
carve	say	go
seek	stand	find
look	fall	grow
swing	blot	cry

Box B		
found	said	cried
looked	sought	grew
swung	went	fell
blotted	carved	stood

C Use three of the **past simple verbs** from **Box B** in sentences of your own.

Planning a story

The **plan** for many stories is the shape of a mountain.

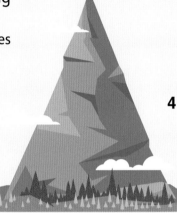

3 Climax: the top of the mountain is in the middle of the story when things get most difficult, frightening or exciting!

2 Build-up: from the beginning to the middle of the story, characters may find themselves in a difficult situation.

1 Introduction: at the beginning of the story, readers are at the foot of the mountain. They find out the setting for the story and meet the characters.

4 Resolution: from the middle to the end things are sorted out, although they don't always turn out well!

1   Look for the mountain shape in the extract from *Erik the Viking* on **pages 14 and 15**. Make brief **notes** about:

   a   the **introduction**   b   the **build-up**

   c   the **climax**   d   the **resolution**

2   Here is a simple plan for a story about a character called Hiran, who makes a journey by car to visit his brother.

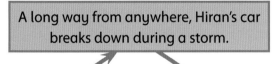

A long way from anywhere, Hiran's car breaks down during a storm.

Hiran sets out to visit his brother.

Hiran arrives at his brother's house.

Make **notes** on:

   a   how the story will begin – the introduction

   b   the things that go wrong for Hiran – the build-up

   c   when things are as bad as they can get – the climax

   d   how Hiran's problems are sorted out – the resolution.

A Chinese Play

Long, long ago, in a Chinese town, there lived a judge called Judge Wang. When the people of the town had disagreements, they would go to the judge. He would decide who was in the right and who was in the wrong. He was, however, not a fair judge. He would only help people if they agreed to pay him lots of money.

The Painter and the Judge

Characters: JUDGE WANG: an important but dishonest person in the town

PAINTER: a very talented man who visits the town

Scene 1: *A riverbank. It is just after **sunrise**. A painter is painting a picture of the river. The judge arrives carrying a roll of white paper.*

JUDGE: [*cheerily*] Good morning my fine fellow! I am the judge in this town and I am very important! I have heard that you are a painter with great talent. I want you to paint a picture for me. I will pay you handsomely!

PAINTER: [*aside*] I have heard all about this judge and how he cheats people. I could spend a lot of time on this painting but probably not get paid!

[*aloud*] I am sorry judge, but as you can see, I am very busy at the moment.

Glossary

scene part of a play
sunrise when the sun comes up
aside words that are spoken to the audience so other characters on stage cannot hear

JUDGE:	Nonsense! I am sure you can find the time. If you paint me a beautiful picture, I will put it up in my house. Many important people visit me. They will all see the painting and you will get more work.
PAINTER:	Well, even if I could find the time, the painting would be very expensive. I'm not sure you could afford it.
JUDGE:	[*impatiently*] I have lots of money. I can afford anything! Now, no more excuses. Here is the paper. Get on with it!

Scene 2:	***Later that day. The painter is standing in a beautifully furnished room in the judge's house. He is carrying the roll of paper. The judge enters.***
PAINTER:	Good afternoon, Judge Wang. I have finished the painting.
JUDGE:	Wonderful! Wonderful! I can't wait to see it. [*The judge snatches the paper from the painter's hand and unrolls it. He reads.*] A herd of goats on grass.
PAINTER:	That's the title of the painting.
JUDGE:	[*puzzled*] Well, yes, but where's the painting? Apart from the title, there's nothing there! There is no grass.
PAINTER:	[*very seriously*] Well, the goats had a good feed and all the grass is gone.
JUDGE:	[*bewildered*] So, where are the goats?
PAINTER:	Well, obviously, as there was nothing left to eat, the goats left to find another field.
JUDGE:	[*really angry*] I'm not paying you for this blank sheet of paper!
PAINTER:	Fair enough! I didn't expect to get paid anyway! [*The painter leaves smiling.*]

Word Check

> You can use a dictionary to help you.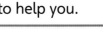

A   Find each word in the passage.
Choose the correct meaning.

   1 talented   **a** wealthy   **b** skilful

   2 expensive   **a** cheap   **b** costing a lot of money

B   Find these phrases in the story. Discuss what they mean.

   1 pay you handsomely   **2** no more excuses

Comprehension

A Discuss the answers to these questions.

    1 How many characters are there in the play?

    2 How many scenes are there?

    3 Where is the first scene set?

    4 Where is the second scene set?

B Write a sentence to answer each question.

    1 What words and phrases could you use to describe:

        a the character of Judge Wang?

        b the painter?

    2 Why does the painter tell the judge that he is 'very busy'?

    3 Why does the painter say 'I didn't expect to get paid anyway'?

    4 Do you think the painter was being fair or unfair when he did not paint a picture for the judge? Explain your reasons.

C Why do you think the play is in **two** scenes?

A herd of goats on grass

Vocabulary

Alphabetical order

It is easy to find a word in a dictionary because the words are arranged in **alphabetical order**.

> **attractive** *adj* very pleasant to look at
> **audience** *n* people who have come to a play, a concert or a talk
> **August** *n* the eighth month of the year
> **aunt**, **auntie** *n* 1. a sister of your father or mother
> 2. your uncle's wife

A Write each group of letters in alphabetical order.

1 b d c a

2 t v w u

3 i g f h

4 W u x V

5 h j e r w z

6 l d t m w s

7 G H S Y E Q

8 J O L B V F

9 X S A P M C

10 P N F J Y E

B Write these words in alphabetical order.

1 pond house garden

2 stream sad suddenly sent

3 minute merry marry

4 winner wall weep worry

5 river rain roll read

6 people play picture painter

> Remember, if the words begin with the same letter, you need to look at the second letter in each word.

Dialogue in plays

Remember, when we write **dialogue** in **stories** we use **speech marks**.

"Good morning," said the judge.

When we write **dialogue** in a **play**, we set it out differently.

JUDGE: Good morning.

name of character   spoken words

We do **not** use speech marks or words like **said**.

A Write these direct speech sentences as they **would appear in a play**.

The first one is done for you.

1 "What are you painting?" asked the judge.
   JUDGE: _What are you painting?_

2 "I am painting a picture of the river," replied the painter.

3 "It is very good," said the judge. "I know you have great talent."

4 "Thank you," said the painter.

5 "Would you paint a picture for me?" asked the judge. "I will pay you handsomely."

ive word ending

> Remember, a **suffix** is a word ending. The suffix **ive** usually comes after an **s** or a **t**.
>
> Well, even if I could find the time, the painting would be very expen**sive**.

A Write a word from the word box to match each picture.

massive	expensive	positive	competitive
aggressive	exclusive	inquisitive	relative

1

2

3

4

5

6

B Two of the words in the word box haven't been used in **Activity A**. Write each of them in a **sentence**.

C Copy the words, adding **ive** to make each word into an adjective. Then write a definition for each word.

> Use a dictionary to check your definitions.

1 effect_____   **2** secret_____

3 act_____   **4** creat_____

5 impress_____   **6** decis_____

7 talkat_____   **8** posit_____

Grammar

Noun round-up

> **Nouns** are naming words.

There are different types of **nouns**.

- A **proper noun** begins with a **capital letter**.
  Judge Wang

- A **common noun** begins with a **small letter**.
  picture

- A **collective noun** is the name of a **group of things**.
  a **flock** of birds

- A **compound noun** is made up of two words.
  riverbank

Most nouns are the names of things you can see and touch.
Abstract nouns are the names of things you cannot see or touch.
They are the names of **qualities**, **feelings** or **times**.

   kindness, pleasure, evening

Abstract nouns can be made from:

- common nouns   hero   **heroism**
- adjectives   kind   **kindness**
- verbs   to please   **pleasure**

A Copy the sentences. Underline the **abstract noun** in each sentence.

1 The woman praised his talent.

2 The man lived in poverty.

3 The judge guarded his wealth.

B Write the **abstract noun** that can be made from each of these.

> You can use a dictionary to help you.

1 common nouns **a** infant   **b** child   **c** adult

2 adjectives   **a** brilliant   **b** miserable   **c** wise

3 verbs   **a** to know   **b** to please   **c** to fail

C Use three of the abstract nouns you have formed in **Activity B** in sentences of your own.

Play scripts

Long plays are divided into **acts**, like the chapters of a book. Each act has several **scenes**. Shorter plays, like *The Painter and the Judge*, just have **scenes**.

Plays have:

- a **title**

  The Painter and the Judge

- **characters** – the people in the play. The list of characters at the beginning of a play gives the names and describes who they are.

  JUDGE WANG: an important but dishonest person

- **settings** – where the scenes take place.

  A riverbank

- **dialogue** – the words spoken by the actors.

  PAINTER: **That's the title of the painting.**

- **stage directions** – notes to show the actors how to say their lines and what actions to do.

  [*impatiently*]   [*The painter leaves smiling.*]

1   You are going to plan a short play that has **two** scenes. You can base your play on:

- you and your friends   • a favourite story   • your own idea

a Think of a **title** for your play.

b Write a list of **characters** in your play and who they are.

c Make notes for **Scene 1**:

- Where is the scene set?

- What happens?

d Make notes for **Scene 2**:

- Where is the scene set?

- What happens?

A Must-See!

If you are lucky enough to visit China, the Great Wall of China is not to be missed! Stretching more than 20,000 kilometres between Gansu in the west to the Yellow Sea in the east, the wall forms a barrier that has existed for over 2,200 years.

Described as one of the **Seven Wonders of the Medieval World**, it attracts over 10 million visitors each year. The first parts of this huge wall were built of stone, wood and earth. It is the longest structure ever built by humans, but if you have read that it can be seen from the Moon, it is untrue!

Visitors stand and stare in amazement, finding it hard to believe that such a structure could have been created in the third century BCE.

Glossary

Seven Wonders of the Medieval World amazing buildings and other structures from early times

Emperor Qin Shihuangdi the ruler of China from 221 to 210 BCE

Manchu people living in the north east of China

Emperor Qin Shihuangdi ordered the wall to be built to prevent invasions from the north.

Such a wall needed gates for people and goods to pass through, and these gates became centres where people settled. In the end, it was one of these gates, opened by a traitor, that allowed the **Manchu** to invade, but not until 1,000 years after the wall had been built.

If you ever have the opportunity to visit the Great Wall, it will be a truly unforgettable experience!

Word Check

You can use a dictionary to help you.

A Find each word in the article. Choose the correct meaning.

    1 barrier   **a** a way of keeping people out

                  b a way of letting people in

    2 structure **a** something grown

                  b something built

    3 prevent   **a** stop   **b** help

    4 traitor   **a** a friend   **b** an enemy

B Find these phrases in the story. Discuss what they mean.

    1 not to be missed

    2 people settled

    3 unforgettable experience

Comprehension

A Discuss the answers to these questions.

    1 Where does the wall start in the west?

    2 Where does it finish in the east?

    3 Who ordered the wall to be built?

    4 Why was the wall built?

    5 How did the Manchu manage to invade China?

The Great Wall of China

Location: North-eastern China, along the Mongolian Plateau

Age: more than 2,200 years

Highest point: approximately 8 metres

Length: approximately 21,000 kilometres

Widest part: approximately 9 metres

Number of lookout towers: approximately 7,000

Built from: stone, soil, sand, brick

lookout tower

ramparts

Glossary

ramparts parts of a wall that can be walked along

lookout towers high places where guards can watch to see if anyone is coming

Word Check

You can use a dictionary to help you.

Find each word in the fact file. Choose the correct meaning.

1 location

   a the place where it is   **b** the length of it

2 plateau

   a mountain   **b** high, flat land

3 approximately

   a about   **b** exactly

Comprehension

B Discuss the answers to these questions.

1 Why do you think the Great Wall of China has so many lookout towers?

2 Why was the wall built using materials like stone and brick?

3 Why do you think it is hard to say exactly how old the wall is?

C Both the magazine article and the fact file about the Great Wall of China are **non-fiction**. They both give the reader facts, but they are very different.

  1 Which would you read if you wanted to know some basic facts about the Great Wall of China?

  2 Which would you read if you were thinking of going on holiday in China?

  3 Do you think the illustrations are useful? Explain your reasons.

Vocabulary

Alphabetical order

Remember, if you are sorting words into **alphabetical order**, and they begin with the same letter, you need to look at the second letter of each word.

baboon   bear   birds   boar   buffalo

a b c d e f g h i j k l m n o p q r s t u v w x y z

If the second letters are the same, you need to look at the third letters.

chair   chess   China   choir   chutney

a b c d e f g h i j k l m n o p q r s t u v w x y z

A Sort these words into alphabetical order.

> The words in a dictionary are in alphabetical order.

  1 chestnut   charcoal   churn   chick

  2 herd   heap   hexagon   help

  3 month   moth   moss   mole

  4 wall   warm   wafer   wake

B Write your own short definition of each of these words.

  1 create   **2** amazement   **3** traitor

  4 visible   **5** invade   **6** location

C Use a dictionary to find the correct definition of each word from **Activity B**. Copy the definitions.

Commas in lists

> When we write a **list** in a sentence we use **commas**. We join the last two things in the list with **and**, **but** or **or**.
>
> The first parts of this huge wall were built of stone, wood and earth.

A Copy the sentences. Add the missing commas.

1 We could visit China India or Thailand.

2 The wall is long high and wide.

3 I visited India, Sri Lanka and Pakistan but not China.

B Add the commas and the missing word **and**, **but** or **or** to the following sentences.

1 The Great Wall of China is built from stone sand soil _____ brick.

2 We can visit the Great Wall of China the Yangtze River _____ the Forbidden City.

3 The gates let through people goods _____ not traitors.

C Use each of the words provided below in a sentence of your own. Include a list using commas and the word **and**, **but** or **or**.

1 train plane boat bike

2 pandas lions bears crocodiles

3 river city mountain forest

Spelling

ea words

> The letters **ea** can make a number of different sounds in words. In this unit we are looking at the **ea** sound that is found in fe**a**ther.
>
> If you have r**ea**d that the Great Wall of China can be seen from the Moon, it is untrue!

A Find the word in the box that rhymes with the words in these pictures.

1
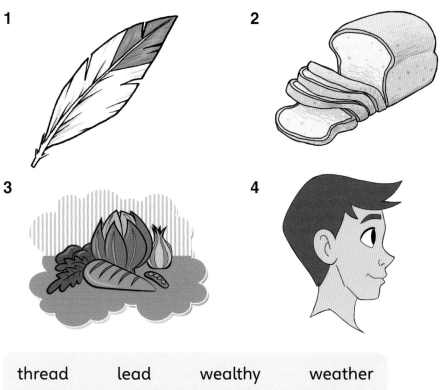

2

3

4

| thread | lead | wealthy | weather |

B Write as many **ea** words as you can that sound like the **ea** in h**ea**d.

8 words = good   10 words = excellent   14 words = FANTASTIC!

C Write three sentences but …

1 the first sentence must have one **ea** word.

2 the second sentence must have two **ea** words.

3 the third sentence must have three **ea** words.

The present perfect tense

Verbs are doing or being words. **Past tense verbs** tell us what people, animals and things **did**.

To make the **past simple tense**, we usually add **ed** or **d** to the verb family name.

Qin Shihuangdi **ordered** the wall to be built.

We make the **past progressive tense** like this:

Visitors **were staring** in amazement!

> To make the **ed** form of a **regular** verb, we add **d** or **ed** to the **verb family name**.

The **present perfect tense** also tells us what has happened in the **past**. We make the present perfect tense of regular verbs like this:

present simple of the verb **to have** + the **ed** form of a verb.

The wall **has existed** for over 2,200 years.
Millions of people **have visited** the wall.

A Which two words make up the **present perfect tense** in each sentence?

1 The Great Wall of China has formed a barrier for over 2,200 years.

2 The gates have allowed people and goods to pass through.

3 The Manchu have invaded China.

B These sentences are in the **present simple tense**. Copy the sentences, changing the underlined verb in each sentence into the **present perfect tense**.

> The first one is done for you.

1 She <u>visits</u> lots of countries.   She has visited lots of countries.

2 He <u>describes</u> how the wall was built.

3 They <u>stare</u> in amazement.

4 The wall <u>prevents</u> invasions.

5 The traitor <u>allows</u> the Manchu through the gate.

C Use these verbs in the present perfect tense in sentences of your own.

1 to look   2 to stare   3 to describe   4 to miss

Factual writing

> **Factual writing** is true and gives the reader **information**.
> There are many different ways of presenting information.
> The way in which **facts** are written depends on their **purpose**.
> Both pieces of writing on **pages 30 and 31** and **page 32**
> are **factual**.
>
> **Magazine article**
> The purpose of the magazine article on **pages 30–31** is to
> encourage people to visit China, especially the Great Wall. The
> article includes:
>
> * information about the Great Wall of China
>
> * why people visit it
>
> * a photograph to show readers what it actually looks like.
>
> **Fact file**
> The purpose of the fact file on **page 32** is to give the reader the
> important facts about the Great Wall. The fact file includes:
>
> * facts about the Great Wall of China
>
> * a labelled illustration to show details of the wall.

1   Choose **one** of the following subjects:

The Great Pyramid of
Khufu – one of the Great
Pyramids of Egypt

Victoria Falls – magnificent
waterfalls at the border
of Zambia and Zimbabwe

Petronas Towers –
a skyscraper in Kuala
Lumpur, Malaysia

Research your chosen subject and make a **fact file** of the important
information about the place.

2   Use the facts you researched in **Activity 1** to write **an article for a travel
magazine**. You should include:

* information about the place

* a description that will encourage readers to visit.

Castles in Stories

Some very exciting stories are set in the past and take place in castles. Some of the castles are beautiful and welcoming – some are dark and scary! This is part of a story by the Brothers Grimm where a poor fisherman and his wife are given a beautiful castle to live in.

The Fisherman's Castle

It was a huge stone castle with dark green ivy growing up the walls. There was a grand staircase and a hundred rooms. All the rooms had beautiful furniture. The chairs and tables were made of gold. Behind the castle there was a lovely garden and a huge wood. From the high windows, they could see sheep, goats, hares and deer in the castle grounds. In the **courtyard** there were stables for horses. It really was a wonderful and peaceful place.

Glossary

courtyard an outdoor area surrounded by buildings

Word Check

You can use a dictionary to help you.

A Find each word in the story. Choose the correct meaning.

1 huge	**a** very big		**b** very small	
2 grand	**a** impressive		**b** unimpressive	
3 wonderful	**a** amazing		**b** boring	
4 peaceful	**a** noisy		**b** calm	

Comprehension

A Discuss the answers to these questions.

1 What was growing on the walls of the castle?

2 How many rooms were there?

3 What were the chairs and tables made of?

4 Make a list of the animals that could be found around the castle.

5 Find an adjective used to describe:

    a the castle   **b** the staircase   **c** the furniture

    d the garden   **e** the wood   **f** the windows

B Imagine you are the fisherman or his wife. Carefully read the description of the castle and write a few sentences to describe how you **felt** and what you **did** when you first saw the castle.

This castle appears in *The Snow Queen* by Hans Christian Andersen. Gerda, one of the characters in the story, is taken to the castle.

The Snow Queen's Castle

Suddenly the carriage stopped. They had reached the courtyard of the castle. Its walls were cracked from top to bottom. Crows and **ravens** were flying out of the gaps and holes. Huge **hounds**, each one looking as if it could swallow a man, leapt high in the air, but not a single bark came from them for that was forbidden. In the great old hall, cobwebbed and black with **soot**, a large fire burned on the stone floor. The smoke drifted about under the roof, trying to find its way out. A vast **cauldron** of soup was bubbling away …

Glossary

ravens large black birds
hounds a type of dog
soot black dirt from a fire
cauldron a large cooking pot

39

A Find each word in the *The Snow Queen's Castle* story on **page 39**. Choose the correct meaning.

1	suddenly	**a** without warning		**b** noisily
2	leapt	**a** floated		**b** jumped
3	forbidden	**a** allowed		**b** not allowed
4	vast	**a** big		**b** hot

Comprehension

A Discuss the answers to these questions.

1 Where did the carriage stop?

2 What were the crows and ravens doing?

3 What did the hounds do?

4 What was in the cauldron?

5 Find a word or phrase used to describe:

  a the castle walls   **b** the hounds   **c** the hall

  d the fire   **e** the floor   **f** the cauldron

B Imagine you are Gerda and have been taken to the Snow Queen's castle. Write a few sentences to describe how you **felt** and what you **did** when you first saw the castle.

Vocabulary

Gender words

Remember, **gender words** tell us whether a person or animal is male or female. Words about males are called **masculine words** and words about females are called **feminine words**.

Feminine words often have the suffix **ess**.

  lion**ess**

A Write the masculine form of each of these words.

> Remember, a suffix is a group of letters that goes on the end of a word to make a new word.

1 princess   **2** heiress

3 actress   **4** duchess

5 waitress   **6** headmistress

Some words are both masculine and feminine. For example:

    parent   **you**   **bird**

These are called **common gender words**.

B Draw a table like the one below and write each word from the box under the correct heading.

she	they	him	we
baby	brother	mare	cockerel
sister	foal	uncle	aunt

Masculine	Feminine	Common

C Add three more words to each column of the table you drew for **Activity B**.

Punctuation

Singular possessive nouns

Possessive nouns tell you who **owns** something.
Singular possessive nouns have an **apostrophe** and an **s** at the end.

    The Fisherman**'s** Castle = the castle belonging to the fisherman

    The Snow Queen**'s** Castle = the castle belonging to the Snow Queen

A Write these **singular owners** with an **apostrophe**.

The first one is done for you.

1 the rooms furniture   <u>the room's furniture</u>

2 the fishermans home

3 the castles gardens

4 the walls cracks

5 the fires smoke

6 the halls cobwebs

Spelling

f/fe word endings

> Remember, it can be tricky to make the plural forms of nouns that end with **f** or **fe**. We usually change the **f** or **fe** to **v** and add **es**.
>
> wol**f**   wol**ves**
> wi**fe**   wi**ves**
>
> When a word ends with **ff**, we just add **s**.
>
> cu**ff**   cu**ffs**

A Write the answer to each clue. The answers are all plurals. The singular form of each answer ends in **f** or **fe**.

1 L_____ sometimes fall off trees.

2 K_____ are used with forks.

3 Bread dough is formed into l_____.

4 People who steal are called t_____.

5 S_____ keep our necks warm.

6 You can keep books on s_____.

7 A whole is made up of two h_____.

8 W_____ are large, wild dogs.

> Remember, most spelling rules have some exceptions.
> A few **f/fe** words have plurals that end in **s**.
>
> sa**fe**   sa**fes**
> che**f**   che**fs**

B Write the plural of each word.

Check the words you aren't sure about in a dictionary!

1 life		**2** safe		**3** cliff	
4 giraffe		**5** yourself		**6** chef	
7 shelf		**8** cuff		**9** belief	

Grammar

Adjectives

Adjectives add detail and interest to your writing.

> Remember **adjectives** tell us more about nouns. They can tell us about the shape, size, colour and many other things.
>
>   **stone** castle   **green** ivy   **huge** hounds
>
> Sometimes we need more than a single **adjective** to give a description. We can use an **adjective phrase** to give the reader a clearer picture.
>
> The castle was **huge**.
> **huge** = single adjective
>
> It had **very high stone** walls.
> **very high stone** = adjective phrase
>
> Its walls were **cracked from top to bottom**.
> **cracked from top to bottom** = adjective phrase

A **phrase** is a group of words that does not make sense on its own.

A Look at the story extracts on **pages 38 and 39**. Find a suitable noun for each adjective.

1 golden		**2** menacing		**3** crumbling	
4 squawking		**5** blazing		**6** black	

B Copy and underline the **adjective phrase** in each sentence.

1 The castle had a very beautiful garden.

2 The hounds, huge and silent, leapt in the air.

3 There was a cauldron of soup in the old, black, cobwebbed hall.

C Use these **adjective phrases** in sentences of your own.

1 bright and shiny   2 beautiful and peaceful

3 cracked, dirty and crumbling   4 blazing, crackling and hot

Writing

Settings for stories

Remember, before you begin to write a **story**, you need to plan where the story takes place. This is called **the setting**.

- The setting for part of *The Fisherman's Castle* is a stone castle with a hundred rooms, beautiful furniture, a lovely garden and a huge wood.

- The setting for part of *The Snow Queen's Castle* is an old, crumbling castle with cracked walls and a great hall, cobwebbed and black with soot.

Adjectives and **adjective phrases** help the reader to see what the story **setting** looks like.

1 Look at the **description** of the two castles on **pages 38 and 39**. The way each setting is described has an effect on the reader.

- We feel that the fisherman's castle is friendly and comfortable.
- We feel that the Snow Queen's castle is frightening and uncomfortable.

Imagine you are going to write a **story** called *Trapped*. Choose **one** of these settings:

- a shopping mall
- a forest
- a beach

2 Discuss the **setting** for your story.

a Where are you trapped? For example, it could be a wild forest, a beach on a remote island or a shopping mall after closing time. You may have a better idea.

b What might you see around you? Write a list of **words** and **phrases** that describe where you are trapped.

3 Write **two descriptions** of your chosen setting:

a Your first description must make your reader feel that it is a **friendly, welcoming place**.

b Your second description must make your reader feel that it is a **frightening, dangerous place**.

Let's Celebrate!

New Year Celebrations

New Year is a time for celebrations all around the world, and fireworks have formed a part of those celebrations for years. Many people come together in towns and city centres, thronging the streets to watch the firework displays.

A New Year fireworks display above Big Ben in London, England

Fireworks at the **Burj Al Arab** hotel in Dubai, United Arab Emirates

Celebrations at the Bali Hai Pier, **Pattaya**, Thailand

Fireworks lighting up the sky above the Petronas Towers in **Kuala Lumpur**, Malaysia

Other people like to have small firework parties at home or in their neighbourhood. Family and friends gather to eat, talk and make merry, lighting fireworks as the New Year approaches.

Whether in a public display or private party, fireworks can be dangerous, so there are instructions known as *The Firework Code* that everyone should follow.

Glossary

Burj Al Arab a luxury hotel in Dubai

Pattaya a city on Thailand's east coast

Kuala Lumpur the capital of Malaysia

The Firework Code

How to use fireworks safely

- Only adults should organise firework displays and light fireworks.
- Stand at a safe distance to watch fireworks.
- Keep fireworks in a closed box, away from any naked flame.
- Take fireworks out one at a time then close the box again.
- Read the instructions on each firework by the light of a torch.
- Light all fireworks at arm's length.
- Never return to a firework once it has been lit.
- Never throw fireworks.
- Never put fireworks in your pocket.
- Keep pets indoors.

Word Check

You can use a dictionary to help you.

A Find each word in the passage. Choose the correct meaning.

1 celebrations
   a times for being sad
   b times for enjoying yourself

2 thronging
   a lots of people arriving
   b a few people arriving

3 displays
   a hidden things
   b things for people to look at

4 neighbourhood
   a area where you live
   b gardens

5 code
   a picture
   b set of instructions

B Find these phrases in the passage. Discuss what they mean.

1 make merry
2 at arm's length

Comprehension

A Discuss the answers to these questions.

1 What have been part of New Year celebrations for years?

2 Where do people have small fireworks parties?

3 Where are the following buildings:

　a　Big Ben　　　　　　　b　the Burj Al Arab

　c　Bali Hai Pier　　　　d　the Petronas Towers

4 How many instructions are there in *The Firework* Code?

B Write a sentence to answer each question.

1 Why do people gather in towns and city centres at New Year?

2 Give a reason why you think some people prefer small firework parties at home, rather than a big display.

3 Why do you think fireworks should be kept away from a 'naked flame'?

4 Why does *The Firework Code* say 'Never return to a firework once it has been lit'?

C Discuss:

1 how the instructions in *The Firework Code* are set out.

2 the language and sentences used.

3 the verbs used.

Vocabulary

Words used as nouns and verbs

Words that look the same and sound the same are called **homonyms**.

Remember, a **verb** is an action word and a **noun** is a naming word. Some words can be used as verbs and also as nouns.

Dad is going to **light** the fireworks.　　**light = verb**

Gran turns the **light** off.　　**light = noun**

A Write two sentences for each word, using it as a noun in the first sentence and as a verb in the second sentence.

1 show **2** match **3** box **4** display

B Make a list of some other words that can be verbs or nouns.

Punctuation

Using bullet points

> **Bullet points** help readers to find **important information** quickly. They make it clear where **each item on a list** begins.
>
> • Never throw fireworks.
> • Never put fireworks in your pocket.

A Here are three pieces of information about Malaysia, Thailand and Pakistan. Rewrite them using **bullet points**.

The first one is done for you.

1 Malaysia is in the southeast of Asia. Kuala Lumpur is its capital city. Over 34 million people live there.

• Malaysia is in the southeast of Asia.

• Kuala Lumpur is its capital city.

• Over 34 million people live there.

2 Thailand is in the southeast of Asia. Over 68 million people live there. Bangkok is its capital city.

3 Pakistan is in southern Asia. Over 190 million people live there. Its capital is Islamabad.

Suffixes **ship** and **hood**

> The suffixes **ship** and **hood** are usually just added to the root word. Most suffixes that start with a consonant are added to a root word without changing the spelling of the root word.
>
> Other people like to have small firework parties at home or in their neighbour**hood**.

A Copy these words. Circle the root word and underline the suffix in each word.

1 ownership	2 adulthood	3 partnership
4 championship	5 hardship	6 boyhood
7 motherhood	8 friendship	9 membership
10 falsehood	11 leadership	12 neighbourhood

B Write the word with its correct definition.

1	motherhood	owning something
2	ownership	the period of being a child
3	neighbourhood	a competition to find a champion
4	membership	being a mother
5	childhood	a district in which people live
6	championship	being a member of a group

C Write the following words in your own sentences to show you understand what they mean.

1 partnership   2 adulthood   3 leadership

Grammar

The present perfect tense: regular and irregular verbs

Verbs are doing or being words. **Past tense verbs** tell us what people, animals and things **did**.

> **past simple tense:**   People **watched** the fireworks.
> **past progressive tense:**   People **were watching** the fireworks.

The **present perfect tense** also tells us what has happened in the **past**. We make the **present perfect tense** of **regular** verbs like this:

present simple of the verb **to have** + the **ed** form of a verb. For example:

> Fireworks **have formed** a part of those celebrations for years.

To make the **ed form** of a regular verb we add **d** or **ed** to the **verb family name**.

Some verbs have **irregular** present perfect forms. For example:

> Never return to a firework after you **have lit** it.

> verb: **to light**   present perfect: **has/have lit**

A Copy the sentences. Underline the two words that make up the **regular present perfect tense** in each sentence.

1 We have enjoyed the fireworks.

2 We have gathered to celebrate New Year.

3 He has followed *The Firework Code*.

B Copy the sentences. Underline the two words that make up the **irregular present perfect verb** in each sentence.

1 I have eaten too much!

2 We have taken our pets indoors.

3 She has written about the firework display.

C Change these past simple verbs into **irregular perfect verbs**.

The first one is done for you.

1 I knew   <u>I have known</u>

2 it rang   3 she spoke   4 they broke

5 it blew   6 he grew   7 I gave

Instructions

Instructions are written for many different reasons. They may tell us how to:

- **make** something – for example: a cake
- **do** something safely – for example: watch fireworks
- **mend** something – for example: a bicycle puncture
- **get** somewhere – for example: to find a place of interest.

Instructions have to be:

- easy to understand
- in the correct order.

Instructions:

- often begin with the things you need
- are written in short sentences
- are numbered or bullet-pointed
- are written with the verb at the beginning, telling you what to do or what not to do.

1 Write a clear set of instructions for one of these. Think about what you will **need**. Think about the **order** you do things in.

- building a sandcastle

- making a sandwich

Stig of the Dump

This extract is from a book called *Stig of the Dump*. One day, a boy called Barney goes exploring and makes a very strange discovery.

Far below was the bottom of the **pit**. The dump. Barney could see bits of wreckage among the moss and **elder** bushes and nettles. Was that a steering wheel of a ship? The tail of an aeroplane? At least there was a real bicycle. Barney felt sure he could make it go if only he could get at it. They didn't let him have a bicycle.

Barney wished he was at the bottom of the pit.

And the ground gave way.

Barney felt his head going down and his feet going up. There was a rattle of falling earth behind him. Then he was falling, still clutching the clump of grass that was falling with him.

"This is what it's like when the ground gives way," thought Barney. Then he seemed to turn a complete somersault in the air, bumped into the ledge of the chalk halfway down, crashed through some **creepers** and ivy and branches, and landed on a bank of moss.

His thoughts did those funny things they do when you bump your head and you suddenly find yourself thinking about what you had for dinner last Tuesday, all mixed up with seven times six. Barney lay with his eyes shut, waiting for his thoughts to stop being mixed up. Then he opened them.

He was lying in a kind of shelter. Looking up he could see a roof, or part of a roof, made of elder branches, and a very old rotten carpet, and rusty old sheets of iron. There was a big hole, through which he must have fallen. He could see the white walls of the cliff, the trees and the creepers at the top, and the sky with clouds passing over it.

Barney decided he wasn't dead. He didn't even seem to be very much hurt. He turned his head and looked around him. It was dark in this den after looking at the white chalk, and he couldn't see what sort of

place it was. It seemed to be partly a cave dug into the chalk, partly a shelter built out over the mouth of the cave. There was a cool damp smell. **Woodlice** and **earwigs** dropped from the roof where he had broken through.

But what had happened to his legs? He couldn't sit up when he tried to. His legs wouldn't move. Perhaps I've broken them, Barney thought. What shall I do then? He looked at his legs to see if they were all right, and found they were all tangled up with the creeper from the face of the cliff. Who tied me up? thought Barney. He kicked his legs to try and get them free, but it was no use, there were **yards** of creeper trailing down from the cliff. I suppose I got tangled up when I fell, he thought. Expect I would have broken my neck if I hadn't.

He lay quiet and looked around the cave again. Now that his eyes were used to it he could see further into the dark part of the cave.

There was somebody there!

Or Something!

From *Stig of the Dump* by Clive King

Glossary

pit a deep hole
elder a shrub with white flowers and black berries
creepers long, climbing plants
woodlice small animals which feed on rotten wood
earwigs small insects
yards great lengths of (1 yard is equal to 0.9 metres)

Word Check

You can use a dictionary to help you.

A Find each word in the story.
Choose the correct meaning.

		a		b	
1	wreckage	a	new things	b	damaged things
2	clutching	a	holding	b	cutting
3	somersault	a	turning over	b	jumping down
4	rotten	a	attractive	b	falling to pieces
5	rusty	a	reddish brown	b	shining
6	den	a	rubbish dump	b	secret place
7	partly	a	totally	b	a little bit

B Find these phrases in the story. Discuss what they mean.

1 get at it   2 gave way

3 mixed up   4 tangled up

55

Comprehension

A Copy the sentences, choosing the best word or phrase to complete each one.

1 Barney thought he could see the steering wheel of <u>a car/a ship/a bus</u>.

2 Barney wasn't allowed to have <u>an aeroplane/a bicycle/ a ship</u>.

3 Barney landed on <u>a bank of moss/an old carpet/a rusty sheet of iron</u>.

4 Trees and creepers grew <u>over the mouth of the cave/at the top of the cliff/inside the cave</u>.

B Write a sentence to answer each question.

1 Why do you think Barney wished he was at the bottom of the pit?

2 Why do you think Barney 'lay quiet' after he had fallen?

3 We are told what happened to Barney but not how he felt. Imagine you are Barney and describe your thoughts and feelings when you:

    a are looking over the cliff into the dump

    b have fallen into the shelter

    c thought you might be injured

    d realise you are not alone.

C Look for **words** and **phrases** in the story that describe the pit and the shelter. Copy and complete the word webs.

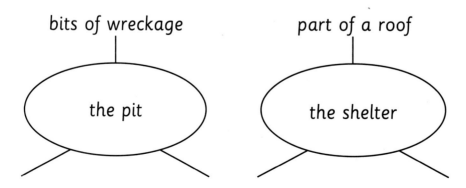

bits of wreckage   part of a roof

the pit   the shelter

Synonyms and phrases

Remember, words or groups of words that have the same meaning, or nearly the same meaning, are called **synonyms**.

And the ground **gave way**.

In the above sentence, instead of **gave way** the writer could have written **slipped away**, **fell away** or **tumbled down**.

A Write a **synonym** for each of the following words.

You can use a thesaurus to help you.

1 bump   2 thinking

3 smell   4 hurt

5 huge   6 den

B Here are some phrases from the story *Stig of the Dump*. Rewrite the phrases using synonyms for the words that are underlined. The first has been done for you.

A **phrase** is a group of words.

1 the ground <u>gave way</u>   *the ground fell away*

2 a <u>rattle</u> of falling earth

3 still <u>clutching</u> the clump of grass

4 the <u>mouth</u> of the cave

Apostrophes of contraction

Remember, **apostrophes** (') are used in **contractions** in place of letters that have been left out.

They **didn't** let him have a bicycle.

The **apostrophe** shows that the letter **o** has been left out.

did n**o**t   didn't

Perhaps **I've** broken them.

The **apostrophe** shows that the letters **ha** have been left out.

I **have**   I've

A Rewrite these pairs of words using an apostrophe.

The first one is done for you.

1 I am   *I'm*

2 you are   3 they will   4 must not   5 let us

B Find four **contractions** in the story on **pages 54 and 55**.

1 Write each contraction as **two words** without the apostrophe.

2 Use each contraction in a sentence of your own.

C Which words could be made into **contractions** in these sentences?

1 Barney should not have gone to the pit.

2 His family would have been worried.

en and on word endings

Most words that end in **on** are **nouns**.
The suffix **en** is often added to a word to make an **adjective** or a **verb**.

Looking up he could see a roof, or part of a roof, made of elder branches, and a very old **rotten** carpet, and rusty old sheets of **iron**.

noun   adjective

A Copy and complete the words that answer each clue. The first one has been done to help you.

1 bones of the body _____skeleton_____

2 adjective to describe something that is gold in colour _____en

3 a type of cloth or thread _____on

4 fastens clothes _____on

5 describes something made of wood _____en

B Add **en** or **n** to each of these words. You may need to double the last letter before adding **en**.

1 hid	2 damp	3 fall	4 red
5 loose	6 bit	7 woke	8 tight
9 short	10 take	11 dark	12 fat

C Look at the answers you have written for **Activity B**. Answer these questions.

1 Write a rule about when to double the last letter before adding **en**.

2 Write a rule about when to add **n** rather than **en**.

3 Write three more words that end in **en** and three that end in **on**. Check your spellings in a dictionary.

Noun phrases

Words that begin **noun phrases** are called **determiners**.

A **noun** is a person, place or thing.

A **phrase** is a group of words that does not make sense on its own.

A **noun phrase** includes a **noun** and **other words** linked to it.

A **noun phrase** can begin with:

| a definite article | **the** dump |
| an indefinite article | **a** bicycle/**an** aeroplane |

a demonstrative adjective:

| singular | **this** ship | **that** den |
| plural | **those** creepers | **these** branches |

A What is the **noun phrase** in each sentence?

1 That cliff is very high.
2 The ground gave way.
3 Those earwigs are falling.
4 Barney wanted that bicycle.
5 This iron is rusty.
6 These woodlice are everywhere!

A noun phrase can be expanded with **adjectives**.

the **damp** smell   a **crawling** earwig

B Make each noun into a **noun phrase** by adding the parts of speech indicated.

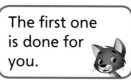

The first one is done for you.

1 definite article + adjective + noun

the chalk cliff

2 indefinite article + adjective + *bicycle*

3 demonstrative adjective + adjective + *creepers*

4 demonstrative adjective + adjective + *shelter*

C Use three of the noun phrases you have written in **Activity B** in sentences of your own.

Setting and characters

> The **setting** of a story affects what **characters** do, say and feel.
> Characters will **act normally** in a familiar, ordinary setting.
> Characters will **act differently** in:
>
> - a familiar setting where strange things happen
> - an unfamiliar setting.
>
> Barney finds himself in an **unfamiliar setting**. Barney is familiar with the top of the pit – but not the bottom!

1   Imagine a large park or garden where you might go to play.

   - Write a **description** of a walk through it and what you would do.

   - Use interesting **adjectives** and **noun phrases** so that your reader can picture the place.

2   Think about walking through the park or garden you described in **Activity 1** and meeting a strange creature.

   Write about:

   - how you felt there was something odd about the place even before you saw the creature
   - what the creature looked like
   - what happened.

Reduce, Reuse, Recycle

Dealing with Waste

Countries all over the world face challenges with rubbish. We throw away many different things.

Type of rubbish	Examples
packaging	cardboard boxes, glass bottles, plastic containers, tins, sweet wrappers
paper	newspapers, magazines, envelopes, junk mail
garden waste	weeds, grass cuttings, dead plants
food waste	potato skins, fruit peelings, leftovers
electrical waste	broken televisions, out-of-date computers

It is amazing how much rubbish countries produce each year. Here are some examples.

Country	Approximate amount of rubbish each year
China	254 million tonnes
United States of America	220 million tonnes
Britain	100 million tonnes
India	60 million tonnes
Thailand	27 million tonnes
Pakistan	20 million tonnes

So what happens to all this rubbish?

In the past, huge holes in the ground were used and all the people's rubbish was tipped into them. These holes are called landfill sites. They are unhygienic and unsightly. They are still used today but some have been improved. The holes are lined so that the rubbish does not contaminate the soil or **ground water**. But there is still a problem. There is just too much rubbish and not enough holes to put it all in!

Glossary

ground water water that flows or collects under the ground

recyclable can be used again

non-recyclable cannot be used again

compostable can rot and be used to fertilise soil

What are governments doing?

All over the world, governments are looking for other, cleaner solutions by providing households with more than one rubbish bin. A household's rubbish can then be separated into **recyclable**, **non-recyclable** and **compostable** material before it is taken away. Some schools also offer classes about recycling. The classes' aims are to make children aware of what can and can't be recycled.

What can we do?

Everyone can help solve this problem by remembering *the three Rs*.

✔ reduce   Help reduce the amount of rubbish that goes into landfill sites. Do not buy items with lots of packaging.

✔ reuse   Instead of throwing things away, try to find another way to use them. Donate clothes and unwanted items to charity.

✔ recycle   Put all recyclable rubbish in a recycling bin. It can then be taken to a recycling plant where it can be made into something that can be used again.

Word Check

You can use a dictionary to help you.

A Find each word in the extract. Choose the correct meaning.

		a	b
1	unhygienic	a clean	b dirty
2	unsightly	a lovely to look at	b horrible to look at
3	improved	a made better	b made worse
4	contaminate	a make something unhealthy	b make something healthy
5	solutions	a ways of making problems	b ways of solving problems
6	reduce	a make more	b make less
7	donate	a take from	b give to

Comprehension

A Discuss the answers to these questions.

   1 Give three examples of different types of rubbish.

   2 Of the countries in the table, which one has:

      a the most rubbish each year?

      b the least rubbish each year?

   3 Where did all the rubbish go in the past?

   4 How have landfill sites been improved?

B Write a sentence to answer each question.

   1 Why do you think 'governments are looking for other, cleaner solutions'?

   2 Why are households 'given more than one rubbish bin'?

   3 Why do you think it is important for children to learn about recycling?

   4 Do you think *reduce, reuse, recycle* is a good idea? Why? Why not?

C The **information** is presented in **three ways**:

   • text   • tables   • photographs

   1 How is information presented about:

      a different types of rubbish?

      b the amount of rubbish thrown away by different countries each year?

      c what governments are doing about it?

      d what you can do about it?

   2 Are the photographs useful? Why? Why not?

   3 Are the sub-headings useful? Why? Why not?

Vocabulary

Over-used word: nice

> **Nice** is one of the most over-used words in the English language. You can usually find a better word to use.
>
>   The smell of the rubbish was not **nice**.
>
> can change to:
>
>   The smell of the rubbish was not **pleasant**.
>
> or:
>
>   The smell of the rubbish was **revolting**.

In medieval times, 'nice' used to mean 'stupid' or 'silly'!

A Copy the paragraph below. Replace each **nice** with a word from the box, or a word of your own, if you prefer.

It was a <u>nice</u> day. Our <u>nice</u> teacher suggested that it would be <u>nice</u> if we went outside for a <u>nice</u> break. She said it would be <u>nice</u> to make the school look <u>nice</u> by collecting the rubbish. It is not <u>nice</u> when people drop litter, but it was not <u>nice</u> for us going to pick up their rubbish. I hope our <u>nice</u> teacher doesn't give us a <u>nice</u> treat like that again!

pleasant	warm	sunny	kind	clean	fun
thoughtful	friendly	sensible	enjoyable	useful	short
relaxing	lovely	brief	good	helpful	tidy

B Choose three of the words from the box in **Activity A** and use them in sentences of your own.

C Rewrite the sentences you have written in **Activity B**, replacing the words from the box with the word **nice**. Now give your sentences to others and ask them which words they would replace **nice** with. Have they chosen the same words as you?

Punctuation

Plural possessive nouns

> **Possessive nouns** tell you who **owns** something.
>
> **Singular possessive nouns** have an **apostrophe** and an **s** at the end.
>
> a household**'s** rubbish = the rubbish belonging to a household
>
> **Plural possessive nouns** that end in **s** have an **apostrophe** at the end.
>
> the school**s'** aims = the aims belonging to the schools
>
> **Plural possessive nouns** that do not end in **s** have an **apostrophe** and an **s** at the end.
>
> the people**'s** rubbish = the rubbish belonging to the people

A Write these **singular owners** with an **apostrophe**.

1 the towns landfill site

2 the potatos skin

3 the schools classes

4 the bins lid

B Write these **plural owners** with an apostrophe.

> The first one is done for you.

1 the countries problem = <u>the countries' problem</u>

2 the sweets wrappers

3 the childrens rubbish

4 the mens bins

Prefixes **un**, **mis**, **dis** and **re**

> Remember, **prefixes** are groups of letters that can be added at the beginning of a word. They change the meanings of words.
>
> Landfill sites are **un**hygienic and **un**sightly.
> hygienic = clean and healthy
> **un**hygienic = dirty and unhealthy
>
> Remember, when you add a prefix, you just add it, even if it makes a double letter.
>
> **un** + natural = **un**natural
> **dis** + similar = **dis**similar

A Complete these words sums.

1 un + necessary = _____   **2** un + wanted = _____

3 dis + appear = _____   **4** dis + satisfy = _____

5 mis + spell = _____   **6** mis + lead = _____

7 re + appear = _____   **8** re + place = _____

B Below is a table of some common prefixes with their meanings.
Copy the table and add at least two more examples for each prefix.

Prefix	Meaning	Examples
un	not	unhygienic
mis	badly, wrongly	misbehave
dis	reverse, remove, separate	dismount
re	again	recycle

C Write four sentences. In each sentence use at least two words which include the prefix listed.

1 un   **2** mis

3 dis   **4** re

Singular and plural

Singular nouns are made plural in different ways.

Noun	Singular	Plural
For most nouns, add an **s**	bin	bin**s**
For nouns ending in **s**, **ch**, **sh** and **x**, add **es**	cla**ss**	cla**sses**
	wat**ch**	wat**ches**
	bu**sh**	bu**shes**
	bo**x**	bo**xes**
For nouns ending in **f** and **fe**, change the **f** or **fe** to **v** and add **es**	shel**f**	shel**ves**
	kni**fe**	kni**ves**
For nouns ending in **consonant + y**, take off the **y** and add **ies**	famil**y**	famil**ies**
For nouns ending in **vowel + y**, just add **s**	bo**y**	bo**ys**

Some nouns end in the **vowel o**. To make these nouns plural, we usually add **es**.

    potat**o**   potato**es**

For **musical nouns** ending in **o** we just add **s**.

    cell**o**   cello**s**

For nouns ending in **oo**, we just add **s**.

    bamb**oo**   bamb**oos**

A Make these singular nouns plural.

1 hole   2 match   3 loaf

4 fox   5 baby   6 toy

B Make these singular nouns plural.

1 tomato   2 piano   3 photo

4 potato   5 radio   6 volcano

C Copy the sentences. Write **was** or **were** to finish each sentence.

1 The rotten tomatoes _____ thrown into the bin.

2 The volcano _____ erupting.

3 The photos _____ in the drawer.

Writing

Information texts

> When you are writing an **information text**, your **sources** are the places you get your **information**. For example:
>
> * books   * leaflets   * websites
>
> When you are writing an **information text** you should:
>
> * makes **notes** on what **you already know** about the subject
> * find **more information** from different **sources**
> * make **notes** about what you have found out.
>
> Remember that notes:
>
> * should not be written in complete sentences
> * should be key words and phrases.

1 Write these three questions in your book.

What is rubbish?

What are the problems with landfill sites?

How can we reduce the rubbish in landfill sites?

2 Read the information about rubbish on **pages 62 and 63**.

3 Make **notes** under the three questions you have written in your book.

4 Add any more information that:

* you already **knew**   * you have **discovered** from other sources

5 Put your notes into **sentences**.

6 Use the questions as **subheadings**.

7 Write three **paragraphs about rubbish**.

8 Give your information text **a title**.

Rainbow Poems

There are many different poems
about the same subject. Here are
two poems about rainbows.

The Rainbow

The rainbow's like a coloured bridge
That sometimes shines from ridge to ridge.
Today one end is in the sea,
The other's in the field with me.

Iain Crichton Smith

Word Check

A Find each word in the poem.
Choose the correct meaning.

You can use a dictionary
to help you.

1	rainbow's	**a** rainbow has	**b** rainbow is
2	ridge	**a** hilltop	**b** sand
3	other's	**a** other is	**b** other has

Comprehension

A Discuss the answers to these questions.

1 What is the rainbow like?

2 Where is one end of the rainbow?

3 Where is the other end of the rainbow?

B Write a sentence to answer each question.

1 Explain what you think 'ridge to ridge' means.

2 Do you think the description of a rainbow as 'a coloured
bridge' is a good one? Why? Why not?

My Rainbow Garden

I have a Rainbow Garden
For inside of it you'll see
Every colour you would find
What a rainbow ought to be.

The blue is for **forget-me-nots**
Yellow for **daffodils**
Red is for my **gladiolas**
My flowers are such a thrill.

Green creates the many leaves
Of my Rainbow Garden too
I get such peacefulness
I would love to show it to you.

My roses, oh I have many
My **palette** of colour shades
I must enjoy them daily
For the time for them will fade.

So if you're feeling weary
And you don't know what to do
Plant flowers of all colours
And have a Rainbow Garden too.

Marilyn Lott

Glossary

forget-me-nots plants with bright blue flowers
daffodils bright yellow flowers
gladiolas tall flowering plants which come in red and many other colours
palette a range of colours

Word Check

You can use a dictionary to help you.

A Find each word in the poem.
Choose the correct meaning.

1	thrill	**a**	excitement	**b**	boredom
2	shades	**a**	sounds	**b**	colours
3	daily	**a**	every week	**b**	every day
4	fade	**a**	die away	**b**	bloom
5	weary	**a**	happy	**b**	tired

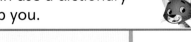

Comprehension

A Discuss the answers to these questions.

1 What does the poet plant for:

   a the blue of the rainbow?

   b the red of the rainbow?

   c the yellow of the rainbow?

2 Which flowers does the poet say have many different 'shades'?

3 If you are feeling 'weary', what does the poet want you to do?

B Write a sentence to answer each question.

1 How does the poet feel when she is in her rainbow garden?

2 Why must she enjoy her garden 'daily'?

C Work out the **rhyming pattern** of:

1 *The Rainbow*

2 *My Rainbow Garden*

Vocabulary

Using a dictionary

There is often a choice of words to use in your writing. Use a dictionary to check the exact definitions of words with similar meanings.

Remember, **synonyms** are words that have the same or almost the same meaning. The exact meaning can be slightly different. For example:

red and **scarlet** are synonyms, but with a slightly different meaning. Red is a colour that includes many different shades. Scarlet is a bright shade of red.

field and **meadow** are synonyms, with a slightly different meaning. A field is an area of open ground, planted with crops or grass. A meadow is a field of long grass and wild flowers.

A Copy each sentence and choose the best word to fit the gap.

Use a dictionary to help you.

1 My friend and I <u>communicated/chatted/whispered</u> on the telephone for an hour.

2 The sun <u>glittered/twinkled/shone</u> brightly in the deep blue sky.

3 I <u>cleansed/washed/scrubbed</u> my hair this morning.

B Write your own definition of each noun below without using a dictionary. You don't have to write a complete sentence.

1 bridge   2 rainbow   3 flower   4 orange

Punctuation

Apostrophes of contraction

Remember, **apostrophes** (') are used in **contractions** in place of letters that have been left out.

    The rainbow's (rainbow **is**) like a coloured bridge.

The **apostrophe** shows that the letter **i** has been left out.

    For inside of it you'll (you **will**) see …

The **apostrophe** shows that the letters **wi** have been left out.

A Rewrite these pairs of words using **an apostrophe**.

The first one is done for you.

1 was not   <u>wasn't</u>

2 there is   3 we shall   4 we have   5 you are

6 did not   7 it is   8 it has   9 would not

B Use three of the contractions you have made in **Activity A** in sentences of your own.

Silent letters

> **Silent letters** can make words tricky to spell. For example:
>
> I am fas**c**inated by rainbows.
>
> However, there are some rules you can learn to help you!
> The letters next to silent letters can often give you a clue.
>
> The silent **c** usually follows the letter **s**. For example:
>
> s**c**ene   s**c**ience
>
> A silent **h** often follows the letters **c** or **r**. For example:
>
> c**h**oir   r**h**yme
>
> A silent **o** sometimes comes before the letter **u**.
>
> d**o**uble   t**o**uch

A Copy the words and underline the silent letter in each word.

1 cousin	**2** chemist	**3** scenery
4 scissors	**5** country	**6** scenic
7 crescent	**8** chorus	**9** young

B For each group of words, write a sentence describing what you notice about the letter that comes before or after the silent letter.

1 scenery	scissors	scent
2 choir	school	chemist
3 country	cousin	young

C Each of these words has a missing silent letter. Rewrite the words correctly.

1 musle	**2** sent	**3** tuch
4 disipline	**5** truble	**6** asend
7 ace	**8** caracter	**9** eco

Grammar

Possessive adjectives and possessive pronouns

- **Possessive adjectives** describe nouns. For example:

  My flowers are such a thrill.

  Possessive adjectives:
my	your	his	her	its
our	your	their		

  Remember, an **adjective** describes a noun.
  A **pronoun** stands in place of a noun.

- **Possessive pronouns** stand in the place of a **possessive adjective + a noun**. For example:

  These flowers are **mine**.   [my flowers]

  Possessive pronouns:
mine	yours	his	hers
ours	yours	theirs	

(A) **1** Copy the sentences and underline the **possessive adjective**.

  a Your roses have a stronger scent than the daffodils.

  b Those daffodils are like the ones in my garden.

  c I can see a rainbow and its colours are very bright.

  d Our park is filled with colourful flowers.

2 Copy the sentences and underline the **possessive pronoun**.

  a That field is ours.   **b** That rainbow garden is hers.

  c Are those daffodils yours?   **d** These red roses are his.

B Copy and complete each sentence with a **possessive pronoun**.

The first one is done for you.

1 This is my flower.   This flower is <u>mine</u>.

2 Is this her garden?   Is this garden _____?

3 That is his rainbow cake.   That rainbow cake is _____.

C Use these **possessive pronouns** in sentences of your own.

1 ours   **2** theirs   **3** yours

Writing

Poetry

The Rainbow on **page 70** is a poem with one verse. It has a rhyme scheme:

lines 1 and 2 rhyme
lines 3 and 4 rhyme

My Rainbow Garden on **page 71** is a poem with five verses. It has a rhyme scheme:

lines 2 and 4 rhyme in each verse

A poem that **rhymes** must also **make sense**.
The poet thinks of rhyming words and picks the ones that make the best sense.

The rainbow's like a coloured **bridge**
That sometimes shines from ridge to _____ fridge? ridge?
Today one end is in the **sea**
The other's in the field with _____ bee? free? me?

1 Make lists of words that could complete each pair of rhyming lines.

   a The sun rose up into the sky

      The little clouds were floating _____.

   b The rain pours down, the sky is _____.

      I wish the rain would go _____.

   c The wind was cold and very _____.

      It dragged the swirling leaves _____.

2 Read the words in the box. Sort the **rhyming words** into two lists.

sea	tree	cat	bee
sat	fat	me	that
hat	mat	tea	she

3 Use one of your lists of rhyming words to write a four-line poem of your own. Lines 2 and 4 should rhyme.

UNIT 10 Books About Bridges

Here are three extracts from three different books about bridges.

From *The History of Bridges*

The earliest bridges were made of whatever was available, laid across a stream or river that needed to be crossed. They were often made from tree trunks or large, flat stones.

In Africa and Asia, the earliest bridges may have been very simple **suspension bridges**. These were formed from twisted bamboo or creepers hung across a stream. Their ends would be tied to tree trunks on either side. Bridges like this can still be found in Africa and Asia.

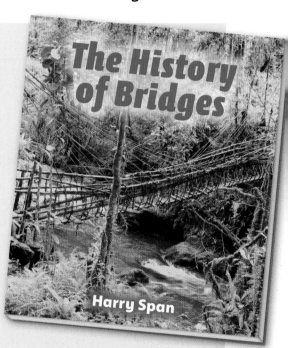

The History of Bridges

Harry Span

From *Bridge Disasters*

Bridges have collapsed for many reasons. Some have been overloaded with people or traffic. Others have been hit by boats going under them. Some have not withstood the weather.

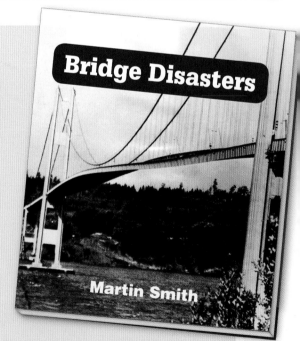

Bridge Disasters

Martin Smith

The Tacoma Narrows Bridge in the USA was a suspension bridge of 1,810 metres. It collapsed in November 1940, just four months after it was completed. People had noticed that, even in a breeze, it moved up and down like the waves in the sea. On November 7th, the wind reached over 60 kilometres per hour and the bridge was twisting and turning alarmingly. At 9.30 a.m., the bridge was closed because it was too dangerous to cross. By midday, most of the bridge had disappeared. All that was left were two giant towers and a mess of **cables**.

Suspension Bridges

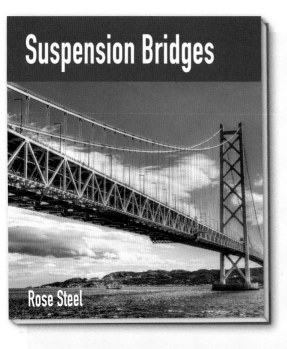
Rose Steel

From *Suspension Bridges*

Many of the longest, modern road bridges over rivers and bays are suspension bridges. Two large **towers** are built, usually of concrete, and steel cables are hung between them. More cables hang down from the main cables, and these 'suspend' the bridge above the water.

The Humber Bridge in England was completed in 1981. At that time it was the longest bridge in the world. Its main **span** was 1,410 metres. Since then, longer and longer bridges have been constructed.

This chart gives details of the five longest suspension bridges in the world, at the present time.

Bridge	Opened	Location	Links	Span
Akashi Kaikyo Bridge	1998	Japan	city of Kōbe to island of Iwaya	1,991 metres
Xihoumen Bridge	2009	China	crosses Xihoumen waterway	1,650 metres
East Bridge	1998	Denmark	Zealand and Funen islands	1,624 metres
Yi Sun-sin Bridge	2012	South Korea	cities of Kwangyang And Yeosu	1,545 metres
Runyang Bridge	2005	China	both banks of the Yangtze river	1,490 metres

Glossary

suspension bridges bridges hung from cables and supported at both ends by tall towers
towers tall buildings at both ends of a bridge
cables long, thick ropes of steel
span the length of the roadway between a bridge's towers

Word Check

A Find each word in the books. Choose the correct meaning.

1 available
  a nearby
  b far away

2 overloaded
  a holding too many
  b holding too few

3 withstood
  a liked
  b resisted

4 alarmingly
  a calmly
  b frighteningly

5 constructed
  a dreamed about
  b built

> You can use a dictionary to help you.

Comprehension

A Discuss the answers to these questions.

1 Which book gives you information on early bridges?

2 In which book would you find information about the Humber Bridge?

3 In which book would you find information about the Tacoma Narrows Bridge?

4 Where is the longest suspension bridge in the world?

5 When was the East Bridge opened?

B Explain in your own words what you understand by the phrases in blue in each sentence.

1 In Africa and Asia, the earliest bridges may have been **very simple suspension bridges**.

2 Bridges **have collapsed for many reasons**.

3 People had noticed that, even in a breeze, **it moved up and down like the waves in the sea**.

4 **At that time** it was the longest bridge in the world.

C Choose either *The History of Bridges* or *Bridge Disasters*. Make **notes** on the text by writing down **key words** and **phrases**.

Vocabulary

Definitions

The word **bridge** has different meanings. Remember, words like this are called **homonyms**.

These are the dictionary definitions for the word **bridge**.

bridge

1 **(n)** a passageway across a river or other barrier

2 **(n)** the captain's platform over a ship's deck

3 **(n)** a card game like whist

4 **(v)** to link two things

n = noun
v = verb

A The words below have more than one meaning. Without using a dictionary, write two definitions for each word, using no more than seven words for each definition.

Remember to say if it's a noun **(n)**, a verb **(v)** or an adjective **(adj)**.

1 trunk   2 cross   3 present

B Now write a definition for each of the words below but use no more than five words for each definition.

1 stream   2 steel   3 suspend

C Check your definitions in a dictionary.

Commas in numbers

Commas are used to make reading **big numbers** a little easier.

The Tacoma Narrows Bridge in the USA was a suspension bridge of **1,810** metres.

Counting from the right, a comma is put in after every three digits.

Note that commas are not used when writing the year something took place. For example: **1981**

1,810   21,810   421,810   1,421,810

A Copy and add the comma or commas in each number.

1 1650 metres   **2** 31650 metres   **3** 531650 metres

4 1545 metres   **5** 21545 metres   **6** 821545 metres

7 1531650 metres   **8** 3821545 metres   **9** 7314210 metres

B Write each of these using **numbers**. Remember the **comma**!

1 one thousand, three hundred and forty eight

2 six hundred and fifty thousand, two hundred and eleven

Spelling

sion, ssion and cian word endings

A very common suffix is **ion**. It is added to many root words.

The suffix **ion** usually has a **t** or an **s** in front of it. This unit covers the suffix with an **s** in front of it.

Remember, **root words** are words to which suffixes or prefixes are added to make other words in the same word family.

In Africa and Asia, the earliest bridges may have been very simple suspen**sion** bridges.

sion is used if the root word ends in **d** or **se**.

suspend/suspension   revise/revision

ssion is used if the root word ends in **ss** or **mit**.

possess/possession   permit/permission

A Find the word in the box that matches each picture.

> percussion   vision   admission   discussion   television   division

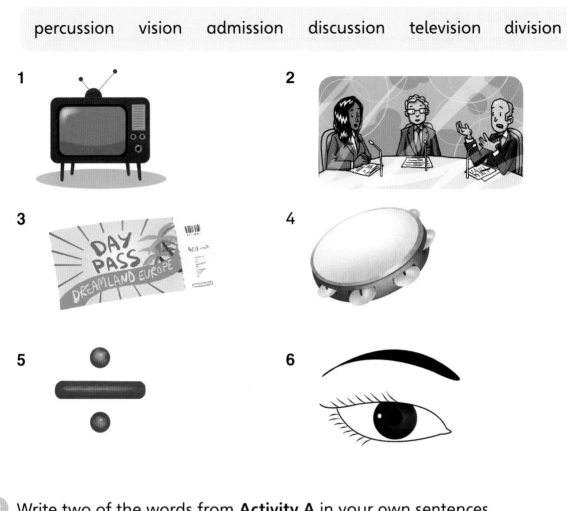

1

2

3

4

5

6

B Write two of the words from **Activity A** in your own sentences.

> The suffix **cian** makes the same sound as **sion**, **ssion** and **tion**.
> It is used if the root word ends in **c** or **cs**.
>   music   musi**cian**

C Add **cian** to each of these to make a word. Say the words aloud.

1 politi_____

2 mathemati_____

3 electri_____

4 opti_____

Grammar

Past perfect tense

When we use verbs to tell us about something that has happened in the **past**, we use **past tenses**.

To make the **simple past tense**, we usually add **d** or **ed** to the verb family name.

Remember! Some verbs do not follow this rule.

> The bridge move**d** up and down. Bridges were form**ed** from bamboo.

We can also use the **past perfect tense**. For example:

> People **had noticed** that the bridge moved.
> Most of the bridge **had disappeared**.

A Copy the sentences. Underline the **past perfect verb**.

1 People had constructed the bridge from large, flat stones.

2 The bridge had collapsed quickly.

3 The wind had reached over 60 kilometres per hour.

4 The cables had snapped.

bank

large flat stones forming a bridge

stream

B Copy and complete each sentence with a **past perfect verb**.

The **verb family names** in the box will help you.

to complete	to overload	to move	to cross

1 He _____ _____ the river using the large, flat stones.

2 The traffic _____ _____ the bridge.

3 The bridge _____ _____ in the wind.

4 She _____ _____ her notes about bridges.

C Use these **past perfect verbs** in sentences of your own.

1 had twisted   2 had turned   3 had disappeared

Collecting information

When you are writing an **information text**, your **sources** are the places you get your **information from**, such as books, magazines or the Internet.

Different sources will give you different information about a subject. The extracts on **pages 78 and 79** come from three books. These books provide information on:

- the earliest bridges
- bridge disasters
- suspension bridges

When you find information in sources, you make notes by writing down **key words and phrases**. If you were looking for information about **what bridges are made of**, your notes might look like this.

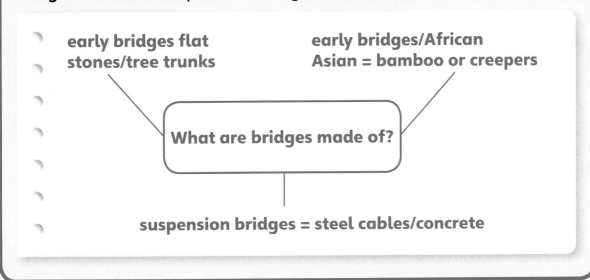

early bridges flat stones/tree trunks

early bridges/African Asian = bamboo or creepers

What are bridges made of?

suspension bridges = steel cables/concrete

---

1   Read the book extracts on **pages 78 and 79** again.

   a Make **notes** on suspension bridges. Remember that your notes should be **key words and phrases**, not whole sentences.

   b Use your notes to write a **short paragraph** about suspension bridges.

2   Look at the picture of the bridge using large, flat stones on **page 84**.

   a Draw an early suspension bridge like those in Africa and Asia.

   b Draw lines to the various parts of your drawing and add **annotations** that will help the reader to understand the picture.

   > We can add short notes to a picture to explain what the different parts of the picture are. These are called **annotations**.

UNIT 11 Robert Louis Stevenson

A biography is a book that somebody writes about another person's life and work. Here is a short biography of Robert Louis Stevenson, author of the adventure story *Treasure Island*.

Robert Louis Stevenson: A Biography

Robert Louis Stevenson was born in Edinburgh, Scotland, on 13th December 1850. His grandfather and his father were **lighthouse engineers**. His three brothers, Alan, David and Thomas, were also lighthouse engineers, and it was thought Louis would follow in their footsteps. In 1867, at the age of 17, Louis went to university to study engineering but he had other ideas about what he wanted to do with his life. He wanted to become a writer.

As a child, Louis was often ill and these problems continued into adulthood. In order to improve his health, he spent as much time as possible abroad in warmer climates, where he wrote about his travel adventures. *An Inland Voyage* (1878) and *Travels with a Donkey* (1879) describe his travels in Europe. *The Silverado Squatters* (1883) describes his time in America. These autobiographical books earned him money for further travelling.

In 1880, Louis married Fanny Osbourne in America. They returned to Scotland with Fanny's 13-year-old son, Lloyd. One day, when the weather was terrible and Lloyd could not play outside, Louis drew a treasure map and began to tell his stepson an amazing tale of pirates, dangerous voyages and hidden treasure. Louis later wrote, "As I pored over my map of Treasure Island, the future characters of the book began to appear there visibly among imaginary woods …"

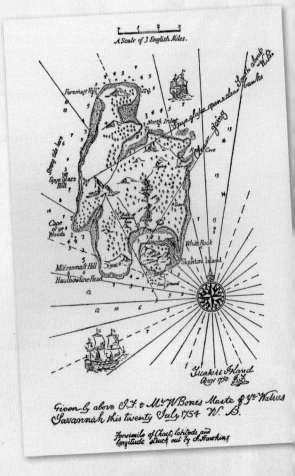

And so, Louis had begun his best-known book, *Treasure Island*! The book was first published as a **serial** in a children's magazine called *Young Folks* from October 1881 to January 1882. It was published as a complete book in 1883. By the end of the 1880s, it was one of the most popular and widely read books. Other exciting adventure stories followed, such as *Kidnapped* (1886), *The Strange Case of Dr Jekyll and Mr Hyde* (1886) and *Catriona* (1893).

By 1888, Louis was restless and in search of adventure. He and his family travelled around the Pacific islands. Louis could not believe the islands were so beautiful. He decided that he wanted to live there. He bought a house on the island of Upolo, the largest island in **Samoa**, and from 1889 until his death in 1894, he lived on his own treasure island.

Robert Louis Stevenson at his house on the island of Upolo, Samoa

Glossary

lighthouse engineers people who build and repair lighthouses

serial a story that is presented in separate parts over a period of time, for example week by week

Samoa a group of islands in the South Pacific Ocean

Word Check

 You can use a dictionary to help you.

A Find each word in the story. Choose the correct meaning.

1	abroad	**a**	in your own country	**b**	in a foreign country
2	visibly	**a**	able to be seen	**b**	invisible
3	popular	**a**	well-liked	**b**	disliked
4	restless	**a**	bored with the way things are	**b**	happy with the way things are

B Find these phrases in the extract. Discuss what they mean.

1 follow in their footsteps   2 autobiographical books

3 pored over   4 widely read

Comprehension

A Write **true** or **false** for each of these statements.

1 Robert Louis Stevenson was born in 1850.

2 He had four brothers.

3 He wrote travel books when he was abroad.

4 Lloyd was Louis's stepson.

5 Lloyd drew a treasure map.

6 *Treasure Island* was published as a complete book in 1881.

7 Louis bought a house in Europe.

8 Louis died in 1894.

B Write a sentence to answer each question.

1 How do you think his father might have felt when Louis said he wanted to be a writer?

2 How do you know that Louis was kind to his stepson?

3 How do you know that Louis had a very good imagination?

4 Why do you think Louis wanted to live on a Pacific island?

C Make a timeline of Robert Louis Stevenson's life, using the dates in the biography. Put the dates in order.

> The first one is done for you.

Date	What happened
1850	Robert Louis Stevenson was born.

Vocabulary

Antonyms

> Remember, an **antonym** of a word has the opposite meaning.
> For example:
>
>   Lloyd could not play **outside**, he had to play **inside** instead.
>
> Some words make the **antonym** by adding the prefix **dis** or **un**.
>
>   Louis **dis**agreed with his father because he was **un**interested in becoming a lighthouse engineer.

A Write down the word that is the antonym of each word below.

1 slowly	drop	crawl	quickly	run
2 praise	sing	criticise	argue	upset
3 success	failure	win	successful	clever
4 exciting	thrilling	strong	sad	dull
5 sharp	cut	blunt	heavy	steel
6 future	past	yesterday	hopeful	vision

B Write the antonyms for each word below by adding the prefix **dis** or **un**.

1 happy   2 certain   3 order   4 helpful

5 friendly 6 concerned 7 connect 8 approve

C Antonyms are sometimes used in **common expressions**. Can you work out what these expressions mean?

1 search high and low

2 take the rough with the smooth

3 from dusk until dawn

4 come rain or shine

Punctuation

Plural and possessive nouns

> Remember, **singular** means one and **plural** means more than one.

When you are deciding whether you need to use an **apostrophe**, you must decide whether a word is:

- a **plural** noun
- a **singular possessive** noun
- a **plural possessive** noun

Many **plural nouns** end in **s**.

His three **brothers** were lighthouse **engineers**.

Singular possessive nouns end in **apostrophe s**.

Lloyd was **Fanny's** 13-year-old son.

Many **plural possessive nouns** end in **s apostrophe**.

The **brothers'** home was in Scotland.

A Which sentences have **plural** nouns? Which sentences have **possessive** nouns?

1 Louis's father was a lighthouse engineer.
2 Louis enjoyed visiting different countries.
3 Louis wrote many books.
4 The island's scenery was beautiful.

B Copy the sentences. Underline the **possessive** nouns and circle the **plural** nouns.

1 Fanny's son liked treasure maps.
2 His father's job was looking after lighthouses.
3 The characters' names are very strange.
4 Louis's books became famous worldwide.

C Copy the sentences and add the missing **apostrophes**.

1 The authors brothers were lighthouse engineers.
2 His brothers names were Alan, David and Thomas.
3 Stevensons dream was to become a writer.
4 The magazines title was Young Folks.

The prefixes **auto**, **super** and **anti**

> Remember, **prefixes** are groups of letters that can be added at the beginning of a word. They change the meanings of words.
>
> **auto** means **self** or **own**   **auto**biographical
>
> His **autobiographical** books earned him money for further travelling.
>
> **super** means **over** or **extreme**   **super**star
>
> **anti** means **against**   **anti**septic

autograph	superhero	anti-clockwise
autocomplete	supercar	antivirus
autopilot	superstore	antibacterial

A Write a word from the word box to match each picture.

1

2

3

4

5

6

B Choose three words from **Activity A**. Write a definition for each word. Check your definition in a dictionary.

C Choose three different words from the word box and write each one in a sentence.

Grammar

Pronouns and possessive adjectives

> **Pronouns** and **possessive adjectives** should be used carefully so the reader is clear about which nouns they refer to. For example:
>
> • Lloyd told Louis **his** map was fantastic.
>
> Does this mean?
>
> | Lloyd had a map. | Louis had a map. |
> |---|---|
> | Lloyd's map was fantastic. | Louis's map was fantastic. |
>
> We can make the meaning clear by using **direct speech**.
>
> Lloyd said, "**Your** map is fantastic, Louis."
>
> • When I was using **my** pen to draw the map, I dropped **it**.
>
> Did he drop the map or the pen?
>
> We can make the meaning clear by **reordering** the words.
>
> I dropped **my** pen when I was using **it** to draw the map.

A What **two meanings** could each sentence have?

   1 The engineer visited his brother on his birthday.

   2 Take the map off the table and clean it.

   3 The woman spoke to the girl while she was writing a list.

B Rewrite these sentences in **direct speech** to make the meaning clear.

> The first one is done for you.

   1 Louis suggested to Lloyd that he could draw a treasure map.

     "You could draw a treasure map, Lloyd," suggested Louis.

   2 Louis's father said he always wanted to be a writer.

   3 Louis's brother said he thought the islands were beautiful.

C **Reorder** the words in each sentence to make the meaning clear.

   1 The boy picked up the map, made a cup of tea and put it on the desk.

   2 When she dropped the glass on the table, it broke.

   3 Before he put the book on the shelf, he dusted it.

Writing

Biographical writing

> A **biography** is the story of a person's life or part of his/her life written **by someone else.**
>
> A **biography** can be:
>
> - a whole book about a particular person's life
> - a shorter account of a person's life in a magazine or on a website
> - a few facts about a person in a dictionary or encyclopedia.
>
> A biography usually begins with the person's birth, and goes **in order** through his/her life.
>
> > Robert Louis Stevenson was born in Edinburgh, Scotland on the 13th December 1850.
>
> > They bought a house on the island of Upolo, the largest island in Samoa, and from 1889 until his death in 1894, he lived on his own treasure island.
>
> A biography contains **facts** about that person's life.
>
> > In 1880, Louis married Fanny Osbourne in America. They returned to Scotland with Fanny's 13-year-old son, Lloyd.

You are going to write a **short biography** about a member of your class.

1 Think about the **information** you will need. For example:

- full name
- when/where born
- where he/she lives
- brothers and sisters
- pets
- likes
- dislikes
- any exciting incidents
- any other information

2 Ask your classmate for this **information** and make **notes.**

3 Use your notes to write a **short biography** of your classmate.

Treasure Island

Robert Louis Stevenson's *Treasure Island* is an adventure story about Jim Hawkins and his search for some hidden treasure.

Jim has found some papers and a book in a sea-chest that was left in his parents' inn by an old pirate named Billy Bones, who has recently died. Some men came to the inn looking for the sea-chest, but they ran away when a group of soldiers arrived. In this extract, Jim goes to see Dr Livesey and Squire Trelawney to show them what he has found.

"First of all," said the **Squire**, "we'll look at the book." Dr Livesey and I peered over the Squire's shoulder as he opened the book. There was some illegible scrawl on the first page and on the other pages there were dates and sums of money.

"I can't make head or tail of this," said Dr Livesey.

"It's very clear to me," cried the Squire. "This is Billy Bones's account book. This is all the money he has stolen from people when he was a pirate!"

We looked at a few more pages. The dates covered 20 years and the sums of money grew larger and larger.

The Squire looked at the papers. The bundle had been sealed with wax in several places. I watched as the Squire broke the seals carefully. One of the papers was a map of an island! It was marked with the names of places where a ship could drop anchor safely near the shore. The measurements written on the map showed that the island was about nine miles long and five miles wide. A hill in the centre of the island was named *The Spy Glass*. **Lines of latitude and longitude** showed where in the ocean the island could be found. There were three large red crosses on the map. Two were in the north part of the island, and one was in the south-west. Next to the last cross were these words: 'Bulk of treasure here'.

Squire Trelawney sprang to his feet. "Well, well," he cried. "You know what we have here?"

"A treasure map?" I said. "A treasure map showing where Billy Bones has hidden all his money?"

"Exactly!" said the Squire, "and we will be the ones to go and find it!"

Dr Livesey said, "That's impossible! How are we going to do that?"

"Nothing is impossible," replied the Squire. "Tomorrow, I will find the best ship I can hire. Jim will come along as **cabin boy**. You must come as well, Livesey. Every ship needs a doctor."

We both agreed. I was excited but frightened too. I remembered the men who had come looking for the **sea-chest**. I was certain they would keep looking. I was certain they would follow us across the sea to the treasure island!

Adapted from *Treasure Island* by Robert Louis Stevenson

A Find each word in the story.
Choose the correct meaning.

You can use a dictionary to help you.

1 peered	**a** glanced at	**b** looked carefully at
2 bundle	**a** a group of things tied together	**b** one thing
3 bulk of	**a** most of	**b** a small amount of
4 sprang	**a** moved slowly	**b** jumped quickly
5 hire	**a** rent	**b** buy
6 certain	**a** very sure	**b** not very sure

B Find these phrases in the story. Discuss what they mean.
1 illegible scrawl   2 sums of money
3 can't make head or tail of   4 drop anchor

Comprehension

A Discuss the answers to these questions.

1 Who left the sea-chest?
2 What does Jim find in the sea-chest?
3 Why does Jim go to see Dr Livesey and Squire Trelawney?
4 What do they find when Squire Trelawney breaks the seals?
5 How many crosses are there on the map?
6 What does Squire Trelawney decide they must do?

B Write a sentence to answer each question.

1 Who is telling the story?
2 How do the characters know that:
   a Billy Bones had lots of money?
   b they have found a treasure map?
3 Why do you think Squire Trelawney 'sprang to his feet'?
4 Why do you think you would need a doctor on board a ship?
5 Why do you think Jim was:
   a excited?
   b frightened?

C Pick out three sentences that show you Jim is telling the story.

Using a thesaurus

> A **thesaurus** is a book that gives the synonyms and the antonyms of a word (if it has any). It may also list other words from the same word family.

> Remember, **synonyms** are words that have the same, or nearly the same meaning. **Antonyms** are words that mean the opposite.

A Find the following words in the extract on **pages 94 and 95**. Use a thesaurus to find some other words that the author could have used instead.

1 arrive   2 find

3 showing   4 near

B Now write an antonym of each word in **Activity A**.

C Copy each sentence, using a thesaurus to help you choose the best synonym to replace each underlined word.

1 Squire Trelawney <u>sprang</u> to his feet.

2 I was <u>excited</u> but <u>frightened</u> too.

3 I was <u>certain</u> they would keep <u>looking</u>.

4 I was certain that they would <u>follow</u> us across the <u>sea</u> to the treasure island!

Punctuation

Direct speech – speaker's name first

Direct speech is when we write the **actual words** someone has said.

For example:

"I can't make head or tail of this," said Dr Livesey.

- We use **speech marks** ("")
  at the beginning and end
  of the spoken words.

- We can use a **comma** (,)
  to separate the spoken
  and non-spoken words.

Sometimes the name of the **speaker** comes first.

Dr Livesey said, "That's impossible! How are we going to do that?"

We **always** use a **comma** to separate the non-spoken and spoken words.

A Copy the sentences. Add the missing **punctuation**.

1 The Squire said It's very clear to me

   The Squire said, "It's very clear to me."

> The first one is done for you.

2 Jim said A treasure map

3 The Squire said Every ship needs a doctor

4 Jim said I am very excited

5 Jim said I think the men will follow us

Spelling

Prefixes **in**, **im**, **il** and **ir**

> Remember, the **antonym** of a word means the **opposite** of a word.

As you know, when a **prefix** is added to a word, it changes the meaning of the word. The prefixes **in**, **im**, **il** and **ir**, when added to words, form the **antonym** of the root word.

There was some **il**legible scrawl on the first page.

"That's **im**possible!"

A Write a word from the box to match each definition.

> inaudible   impatient   illegal   irregular
> incorrect   imperfect   illogical   irresponsible
> invisible   impossible   illiterate   irreplaceable

1 not audible   **2** not visible   **3** not possible

4 not logical   **5** not perfect   **6** not responsible

7 not correct   **8** not legal   **9** not replaceable

10 not regular   **11** not patient   **12** not literate

B Underline the **prefix** in each of the words you have written in **Activity A**.

C Add the correct **in**, **im**, **il** or **ir** prefix to make a word, then write the word in a sentence.

1 ___active   **2** ___legible

3 ___accurate   **4** ___polite

5 ___complete   **6** ___relevant

7 ___formal   **8** ___expensive

Paragraphing in fiction

A **paragraph** is a group of sentences about **one main idea**.
Having **paragraphs** in **stories** makes it easier for readers to follow.
We show a **new paragraph** has started by **indenting** the first line.
We always start a new paragraph when a **different person speaks**.

"I can't make head or tail of this," said Dr Livesey.

"It's very clear to me," cried the Squire. "This is Billy Bones's account book.

We often start a **new paragraph** in a story when:

- the setting changes
- the time changes

We can also start a new paragraph when the setting stays the same but the **characters do different things**.
For example:

The Squire looked at the papers...
Squire Trelawney sprang to his feet...

A Here are some **notes** about what happens next in the story.
Read the notes carefully.

1 next day – Squire Trelawney finds a ship – the Hispaniola – belongs to Captain Smollet – meets Long John Silver – takes him on as ship's cook

2 all the crew arrive – set sail – after some days at sea – see the island – wild-looking – seems to be deserted

3 drop anchor – go ashore – Jim explores the island – meets a wild-looking man called Ben Gunn – been on the island alone for three years

B Use these notes to write **three paragraphs** about what happens next in the story.

Remember that you are telling the story as if you were Jim.

First person narrative

Robert Louis Stevenson wrote *Treasure Island* in the **first person** as if he was Jim Hawkins and the adventure had happened to him.

> **I** remembered the men who had come looking for the sea-chest.

When you are writing in the first person, you should try **not** to begin every sentence with **I** or **We**. This can be very boring!

> I saw the island early one morning. I rushed to the side of the ship. I got into the small boat. I rowed to the shore. I got out. I began to explore.

This piece of writing can be improved by:

- changing the order of the words.
- using conjunctions or joining words (such as: **and**, **so**, **when**, **after, while**)

For example:

> Early one morning, I saw the island **and** rushed to the side of the ship. There was a small boat **so** I got in **and** rowed to the island. **After** getting out of the boat, I began to explore.

1 Imagine you are in the same situation as Jim Hawkins. You have landed on the island and you are exploring. Make **notes**:

- describe what you see
- describe what you do
- describe how you feel

2 Use your notes to write **three paragraphs** about exploring the island. Remember:

- write in the first person
- don't start every sentence with I
- think of interesting ways to begin your sentences.

101

Wildfire

This is part of a story set in Australia. A group of friends are caught up in a wildfire that sweeps across dry grassland. Jan sets out alone in search of her brother Shane, and is separated from the others.

They plunged on. Sometimes they were engulfed in clouds of smoke like stinking yellow mountain mist, but Bill knew the way so well that he went forward unerringly.

Suddenly he stopped. "Listen! A coo-ee!"

The long drawn-out first syllable floated to them on the smoke, followed by the whip-like ending.

"Jan?"

Jan was coo-eeing. It did not sound very loud; there were too many other noises to drown the call.

They listened. Each coo-ee came nearer. It was unlikely that she thought they would be on this track; probably she wanted anyone at all who might be in the **vicinity** to know she was there.

"She's coming back – coming this way!"

Then Jan came out of the smoke. She was crying, and so distraught that she didn't ask how or why they were there. Perhaps she understood. Shane was their friend, too.

"Fire's right across the track! We can't get through!"

"How near?"

"Quarter of a mile, **p'raps**. Not burning as fast now. But creeping up over everything, swallowing everything ... I can't get through. I can't get through to Shane!" Jan was streaked with **grime** and smoke and tears ...

Now they realised that the wind was not altogether subdued by the **cold front**. That a fierce gust had arisen again, and fire was spotting over their heads. ...

It had all the viciousness of fire out of control ... of wildfire.

Bill knew, and the others quickly realised that retreat was cut off.

From *Wildfire* by Mavis Thorpe Clark

Glossary

vicinity the area surrounding a particular place

p'raps perhaps

grime a layer of dirt

cold front a weather term meaning a mass of cold air

Word Check

You can use a dictionary to help you.

A Find each word in the story. Choose the correct meaning.

1 engulfed   **a** surrounded   **b** trapped

2 unerringly   **a** without fear   **b** without any mistakes

3 distraught   **a** happy   **b** upset

4 subdued   **a** frozen   **b** calmed

5 spotting   **a** dropping like rain   **b** going out

6 viciousness   **a** gentleness   **b** violence

B Find these phrases in the story. Discuss what they mean.

1 plunged on   2 whip-like ending

3 drown the call   4 retreat was cut off

Comprehension

A Write **true** or **false** for each of these statements.

1 Bill was unsure of the way to go.

2 Jan was calling because she knew her friends were on the track.

3 Jan had not managed to find Shane.

4 The fire was going out.

5 They could go safely back the way they had come.

B Write a sentence to answer each question.

1 When Jan 'coo-eed', the writer tells us it was not very loud because 'there were too many other noises to drown the call'. What do you think these other noises were?

2 A fierce gust of wind had sprung up. What effect do you think this had on the fire?

3 What evidence is there in the text to show that Jan was very upset about the situation?

4 List the words and phrases the writer has used to describe the fire as a living thing.

C Write a few sentences to explain what you think happens next in the story.

Synonyms for 'said'

When writing dialogue (conversations), we use the word **said** more than any other. Using **synonyms** for **said** can make your writing more accurate and interesting.

"Quick! This way," he **said**.

A more interesting way of saying this might be:

"Quick! This way," he **yelled**.

"Quick! This way," he **gasped**.

"Quick! This way," he **commanded**.

A Make a list of at least ten synonyms for **said** that describe different ways of speaking.

B Copy each sentence below, replacing **said** with a suitable synonym.

1 Suddenly he stopped. "Listen! A coo-ee!" he said.

2 "She's coming back," he said, "coming this way!"

3 Then Jan came out of the smoke. "Fire's right across the track! We can't get through!" she said.

4 "How near?" said Bill.

5 "Quarter of a mile, p'raps. But creeping up over everything, swallowing everything," said Jan.

6 "I can't get through," she said. "I can't get through to Shane."

C Write a short conversation between Bill and Jan using five of the synonyms for **said** that you listed in **Activity A**.

Direct speech – questions and exclamations

> **Direct speech** is when we write the **actual words** someone has said.
> We use **speech marks** around the spoken words.
>
> - If the spoken words are a **question**, we use a **question mark**.
>
>   Bill wanted to know where the fire had got to: "How near?"
>
> - If the spoken words show that the speaker is excited/surprised/worried
>   we use an **exclamation mark**.
>
>   Jan tells them about the dangerous situation: "We can't get
>   through!"

A Copy the sentences, adding an exclamation mark or
question mark in the correct position.

1 "Is that you, Jan" Bill shouted.

2 "I'm so glad you're here"
   Jan cried.

3 "Can we go back the same
   way" she asked.

4 "We must run back now"
   Bill insisted.

B Imagine you are one of the characters in
the story about the wildfire on **page 102**
and you manage to find your friend Shane.

Remember to use
speech marks.

1 What would you say when you
   first saw him?   Use a **question mark**.

2 What would Shane reply?   Use an **exclamation mark**.

3 What would Shane ask you?   Use a **question mark**.

4 What would you reply?   Use an **exclamation mark**.

Spelling

ly word ending

A **suffix** is added **to the end of a root word** to slightly change its meaning.

The suffix **ly** means **in the manner of**.

He stopped sudden**ly**.   **sudden + ly = suddenly**

Remember, because the **ly** suffix starts with a consonant letter it is usually added straight to the root word.

If **ly** is added to words ending in **y**, we change the **y** to an **i** before adding **ly**.

happ**y** + **ly** = happ**ily**

A Add **ly** to each of these words.

1 like 2 quick 3 immediate

4 busy 5 clever 6 careful

7 urgent 8 heavy 9 merry

B Copy the sentences, adding a word from **Activity A** to fill each gap. Each word can only be used once.

1 Bill thought it was _____ that the call came from Jan.

2 He _____ asked the others to be quiet.

3 Jan _____ explained where the fire was now.

4 Bill _____ realised they couldn't go back along the track.

There are some other rules that need to be kept in mind when adding **ly** to a root word.

* If the root word ends in **le**, the **le** is changed to **ly**.
    hum**ble**   humb**ly**

* If the root word ends in **ic**, **ally** is added, not just **ly**.
    trag**ic**   tragic**ally**

C Add the suffix **ly** to each of these words.

1 frantic 2 simple 3 critic 4 possible

Noun and verb agreement

- Nouns and verbs can be **singular** or **plural**. When we use a **singular noun**, we must use a **singular verb**.

    Jan searches for Shane.

    singular noun ⟍ ⟍singular verb

    When we use a **plural noun**, we must use a **plural verb**.

    Her **friends search** for Jan.

    plural noun ⟍   ⟍plural verb

- We use **is/was** with **singular nouns**.

    The fire **is** creeping over everything.

    The fire **was** creeping over everything.

- We use **are/were** with **plural nouns**.

    The children **are** pleased to see Jan.

    The children **were** pleased to see Jan.

A Copy the sentences. Change the **first noun** in each sentence from **singular** to **plural**. Change the **verbs** to match.

1 The animal runs out of the forest.

2 The tree burns fiercely.

3 The bird flies away from the smoke.

4 The firefighter arrives quickly.

B Rewrite these sentences choosing the correct **verb**.

1 Jan is/are shouting to her friends.

2 Jan was/were crying.

3 Shane was/were their friend.

4 Noises is/are everywhere.

C Use each of these **nouns** in a sentence followed by **was** or **were**.

1 fire 2 track 3 friends 4 tears 5 smoke 6 wind

Story endings

> The **ending** of a story is very important. When you plan a story, you must think about how it is going to **end** and what **effect** that ending will have on the reader.

1 The kind of ending you write will depend on how you want your reader to feel. Below are four possible endings for the story on **page 102 and 103**. Each ending will make the reader feel differently. Choose one of these ideas and write an ending for the story.

- **Relief after fear and excitement**

   The children desperately try to escape but they are cut off by the fire. Just when things seem hopeless, they are rescued.

- **Sadness**

   The children escape from the fire but one of them is injured on the way.

- **Surprise**

   A spacecraft from another planet lands and rescues the children!

- **Happiness**

   Heavy rain begins to fall and puts out the fire. No one is hurt.

2 Can you think of a completely different ending for the story? Think about how you want your readers to feel and write the ending.

Fire Beneath Our Feet

Volcanoes

Deep in the centre of the Earth, the rocks are not cold and hard, but extremely hot. This makes them molten like thick **syrup**. This hot rock is called **magma**.

Sometimes magma forces its way up and flows out because it finds cracks in the Earth's crust (outer layer). Magma is called **lava** once it is on the surface of the Earth. The lava gushes out, along with ash and gases, in a fiery mass. The places on the Earth's surface where these **eruptions** occur are called volcanoes.

The lava cools and hardens when it flows down the sides of a volcano. Layers of rock build up and we see the volcano grow with tall, steep sides.

Eventually, cooled lava blocks the opening of the volcano like a cork in a bottle. This is called the plug. When a volcano stops erupting, it becomes **dormant**.

However, old, quiet volcanoes sometimes unexpectedly erupt into life again if magma forces out the plug.

Volcanoes that may erupt again are called active. There are active volcanoes all over the world. Mount Etna in Italy has been active for 3,500 years!

Volcanoes that will not erupt again are called **extinct**. Scientists believe that volcanoes that have not erupted for 10,000 years will not erupt again.

Glossary

syrup a very sweet thick yellow liquid made from sugar
magma hot rock under the Earth's surface
lava hot rock when it is on the Earth's surface
eruptions when volcanoes shoot out lava
dormant sleeping
extinct no longer active

Word Check

You can use a dictionary to help you.

A Find each word in the text.
Choose the correct meaning.

1	molten	**a** runny	**b** hard
2	gushes	**a** flows quickly	**b** flows slowly
3	fiery	**a** cool	**b** hot
4	occur	**a** stop	**b** happen
5	eventually	**a** after some time	**b** immediately
6	unexpectedly	**a** unsurprisingly	**b** without warning

Comprehension

A Copy each sentence, adding words to fill the gaps.

1 Deep in the Earth, the rocks are very _____.

2 This hot rock is called _____.

3 _____ are formed when lava and ash escape at the surface.

4 If a volcano is likely to erupt again it is called _____.

5 If a volcano will not erupt again it is called _____.

B Write a sentence to answer each question.

   1 Why are the rocks in the centre of the Earth 'like thick syrup'?

   2 When does magma become known as lava?

   3 Why is the plug described as being 'like a cork in a bottle'?

   4 Explain the difference between an active volcano, a dormant volcano and an extinct volcano.

C Read the text again carefully.

   1 How many **paragraphs** are there in the text?

   2 Make brief notes on what each paragraph is about. Remember to write down only key words and phrases.

Vocabulary

Synonyms

> Remember, **synonyms** are words and phrases with the same or similar meanings. For example:
>
> **pull** and **tug** are synonyms
>
> Synonyms can be short phrases, too. For example:
>
> **burst out** and **erupt** are synonyms.

A For each word below, write a synonym from the box.

1 molten	melted	solid	thick	heavy
2 centre	circle	middle	edge	corner
3 extinct	fast	find	gentle	dead
4 extremely	very	usually	tiny	slow

Answer the following questions.

   1 Use a thesaurus to find at least three synonyms for each word below.

     a quiet   **b** hard   **c** awful   **d** damage

   2 Choose one of the synonyms for each word in **question 1** and put it into a sentence of your own.

Punctuation

it's or its?

A contraction is a **shortened form**.

The word **it's** is a contraction of **it is** or **it has**.

   Now **it's** [it is] quiet.

   It's [It has] stopped erupting.

Its means **belonging to it**.

   Magma is molten because **its** temperature is very high.

A Copy and complete each sentence with **it's** or **its**.

   1 _____ an amazing sight.

   2 _____ top was glowing with molten lava.

   3 I can't believe _____ happening.

   4 The volcano grew bigger over time and _____ sides became steeper.

   5 When hot rock is on the surface of the Earth _____ called lava.

   6 The lava has gushed out and _____ cooled and hardened.

B Use both **it's** and **its** in one sentence of your own.

Spelling

tion word ending

A very common suffix is **ion**. It is added to many root words. The suffix **ion** almost always has either a **t** or an **s** in front of it.

This unit covers the suffix **ion** with a **t** in front of it. For example:

The places on the Earth's surface where these erup**tions** occur are called volcanoes.

Words ending in **tion** are much more common than words ending in **sion**.

A Find the word in the box that matches the picture.

> addition   direction   calculation
>
> junction   subtraction   section

1

2

3

4

5

6

B Find a word in **Activity A** to rhyme with each of these words.

1 election   **2** attraction   **3** function

Many **abstract nouns** are made by adding **tion** or **sion** to a verb.

If the verb ends in **ate**, the abstract noun will end in **ation**. Notice the final **e** is dropped before adding **ion**. For example:

cre**ate**   cre**ation**

> **Abstract nouns** name things we cannot see and touch.

C Write the abstract noun you can make from each of these verbs.

1 educate	**2** celebrate	**3** situate
4 evaporate	**5** operate	**6** complicate
7 locate	**8** hesitate	**9** separate

Grammar

Adverb clauses

Adverb clauses are **subordinate clauses**. Subordinate means less important.

To make sentences more interesting, we can use **adverb clauses**. An adverb clause works just like an **adverb**. It tells us more about the verb.

An **adverb clause**:

- has a **subject**
- has a **verb**
- begins with a **conjunction**, such as **because**, **when** and **if**
- answers questions such as **why** and **when**.

For example:

The volcano erupted **because the magma had found a crack in the Earth's surface**.

The subject is the person or thing that is doing the action of the verb.

The volcano will erupt **when the magma finds a crack in the Earth's surface**.

The volcano will erupt **if the magma finds a crack in the Earth's surface**.

A Write down the **adverb clause** in each sentence.
1 A volcano stops erupting if the lava blocks the opening.
2 Magma flows out when it finds a crack in the Earth's crust.
3 Magma can flow because it is like thick syrup.

B Copy and complete the sentences with **adverb clauses** of your own.

Begin your adverb clause with **because**, **when** or **if**.

1 We went to see the volcano _____.
2 Volcanoes are dangerous _____.
3 An active volcano is an amazing sight _____.

C Use these **adverb clauses** in sentences of your own.

1 *if I saw a volcano*

2 *when a volcano erupts*

3 *because it is hot*

Writing

Summaries

> A **summary** is a shortened version of something that includes all the **important points**.
>
> To write a summary, you need to:
> - understand what you have read
> - write the important points in your own words.

1a You are going to write a summary of the text on **pages 110 and 111**. Read these **notes** on the first two paragraphs.

> Paragraph 1: centre of the Earth – rocks not cold and hard – rocks = hot and molten – called magma
>
> Paragraph 2: magma comes through cracks – now called lava – brings ash and gases = volcano

1b Read the **summary** of the first two paragraphs written from the notes.

> At the centre of the Earth, the rocks are not hard and cold. They are very hot and molten, and are called magma.
>
> When magma comes through the cracks in the Earth's surface, it is called lava. It brings with it ash and gases. This is a volcano.

2   Now make **notes** on **paragraphs 3 to 7**.

3   Write the **first draft** of your **summary** for **paragraphs 3 to 7**.
Use:
- your own words whenever possible
- the same number of paragraphs.

4   Check your **first draft**. Have you:
- included all the important points?
- used your own words where possible?
- used correct spelling, grammar and punctuation?
- made your summary shorter than the text on **pages 110 and 111**?

5   Write up a final version of your summary.

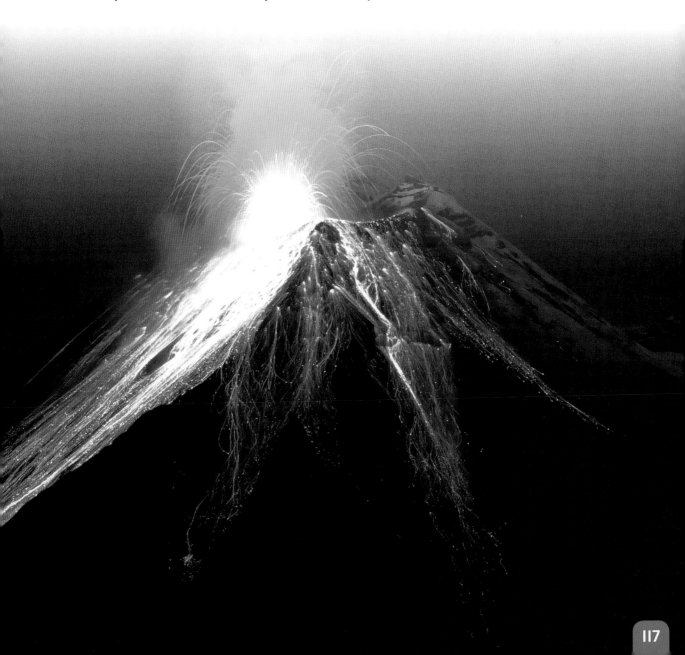

The Mango Tree

Here is an extract from a story called *The Mango Tree* by Madhur Jaffrey. The story is set in India.

In a small town, there was a small house in which lived a young man, his wife, and the young man's sister. This small house had a small garden at the back in which grew a small **mango** tree. One day the young man's wife came to him and said, "Look here, I'm fed up with our **situation**. Your sister …"

"Have you come here to complain about my sister again?"

"What can I do? I know it's quite useless. My complaints fall on deaf ears, anyway … I'm just … so angry with your sister. I get up early in the morning, **draw** water from the well, light the fire in the kitchen, cook breakfast, wash and scrub the pots …"

"Don't go on," said the brother. "I've heard it all before."

"And what does your lazy sister do all day? Nothing … nothing … she lolls about in the garden, watering her mango tree, talking to it, clearing away dead leaves, and feeding it **manure** and **mulch** …"

"That isn't all she does. She comes in and talks to me. Just an hour ago, she was playing chess with me."

"Just because she adores you, doesn't mean you should ignore her faults. You must tell her to leave that … silly mango tree alone, and come and help me with the housework. I really think we should ask her to leave. That might teach her to be more responsible."

Since the sister was old enough to live on her own, the brother could not really object. He knew though, that he would miss her very, very much.

Glossary

mango a sweet yellowish-red fruit
situation the way things are
draw to pull
manure animal dung mixed with soil to help plants grow
mulch a mixture of straw and leaves laid on soil around plants to help them grow

Word Check

A Find each word in the story. Choose the correct meaning.

You can use a dictionary to help you.

1	useless	**a** pointless	**b** important
2	adores	**a** dislikes	**b** loves
3	responsible	**a** sensible	**b** calm
4	object	**a** agree	**b** disagree

B Find these phrases in the story. Discuss what they mean.
  1 fed up **2** fall on deaf ears
  3 lolls about **4** ignore her faults

Comprehension

A Copy the sentences. Add the missing word to complete each sentence.

1 The young man and his wife lived with the young man's _____.

2 The house had a small _____.

3 The wife thought her husband's sister was very _____.

4 Sometimes the sister played _____ with her brother.

5 The sister spent all her time looking after her _____ tree.

B Write a sentence to answer each question.

1 What problem did the young man's wife have?

2 What problem was the young man facing?

3 What words would you use to describe the character of:

  a the wife   **b** the sister   **c** the young man

4 Do you think the solution of asking the sister to leave is the right one? Why? Why not?

C Discuss how you would resolve the problems of the three characters so they could live together happily.

Vocabulary

Diminutives

> In *The Mango* Tree some things are described as 'small' like 'a small house' and 'a small garden'.
>
> A **diminutive** is a word that is formed from another word to describe a smaller version of something. Some diminutives are made by adding a **suffix** such as **ling** or **let**.
>
>   book   book**let**
>
> Sometimes, the root word changes slightly, too.
>
>   goose   gos**ling**

A Write down the word from which each of these diminutives has been formed.

1 nestling   2 spiderling   3 eaglet   4 ringlet

B Write the diminutives of each of these nouns.

> You can use a dictionary to help you.

1 note   2 duck   3 owl   4 drop

> Some diminutives are made by adding a **prefix** such as **mini** or **micro**. For example:
>
>   computer   **micro**computer
>   van   **mini**van

C Using a dictionary, can you find three other words that begin with **mini** or **micro**?

Split direct speech

> **Direct speech** is when we write the actual words someone has spoken.
>
> "Have you come here to complain about my sister again?"
>
> Sometimes we **split the spoken words** with information about who is speaking, so we have to be very careful about the **punctuation**.
>
> "Don't go on," said the brother. "I've heard it all before."
>
> - The brother says **two complete sentences** split by the non-spoken words **said the brother**.
> - Each spoken sentence has **speech marks** at the **beginning** and the **end**.
> - We put a **full stop** after **said the brother** before we begin a new sentence.
>
> "I complain to you," said his wife, "but you never listen."
>
> - The wife has said **one sentence** split by the non-spoken words **said his wife**.
> - Each part of the spoken sentence has **speech marks** at the **beginning** and the **end**.
> - We put a **comma** after **said his wife** before we continue the sentence.

A Copy these sentences. Add the missing **punctuation**.

1 I've come to complain said his wife but I know it is quite useless

2 Your lazy sister does nothing all day said his wife She does nothing

3 She looks after the mango tree said the brother She feeds it manure and mulch

4 Just an hour ago said the brother she played chess with me

5 You must tell her to leave said his wife That might teach her to be more responsible

able and ible suffixes

Two common suffixes are **able** and **ible**. For example:

The wife thought that lazy behaviour was unaccept**able**.

To add **able** and **ible** to a word ending in a single **e**, we nearly always drop the **e** first.

respons**e**   respons**ible**

"That might teach her to be more respons**ible**."

Spelling words that have the suffixes **able** and **ible** can be confusing. Here are two useful tips to help you:

- If you remove **able**, it usually leaves a word that you can recognise. For example:

fashionable   **fashion**

- If the antonym (opposite) of the word is made by adding the prefix **un**, the suffix usually (but not always!) ends with **able**. For example:

unbelievable

A Copy and complete these words by adding **able** or **ible**.

1 avail_____   2 invis_____   3 irrespons_____

4 ined_____   5 reason_____   6 imposs_____

B Add **able** or **ible** to each word.

1 sense   2 wash   3 adore

4 value   5 response   6 break

7 contact   8 afford   9 cure

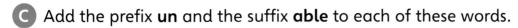

C Add the prefix **un** and the suffix **able** to each of these words.

1 work   **2** use   **3** avoid

4 predict   **5** reason   **6** afford

Grammar

Verb tense round-up

Remember, **verbs** have families.

Verb family names start with **to**.

Verb family name	Verb tense	Examples
to water	present simple	I water/she waters
	present progressive	I am watering/she is watering/they are watering
	past simple	I watered
	past progressive	I was watering/they were watering
	present perfect	I have watered/she has watered
	past perfect	I had watered
	future	I shall water/she will water

Sometimes the verb family members don't look so similar!

Verb family name	Verb tense	Examples
to fall	present simple	I fall/he falls
	present progressive	I am falling/he is falling/they are falling
	past simple	I fell
	past progressive	I was falling/he was falling/ they were falling
	present perfect	I have fallen/he has fallen
	past perfect	I had fallen
	future	I shall fall/he will fall

A Copy the sentences. Underline the **verb** in each sentence.

1 She complains to her husband.

2 Her husband isn't listening.

3 She watered the tree.

4 He was playing chess.

5 She has fed the tree.

6 She had cooked the meal.

7 She will leave the house.

B Copy and complete each sentence, changing the **verb** in brackets into the **tense** given on the right.

The first one is done for you.

1 She (to light) lights the fire.	**present simple**
2 The tree (to grow) _____ in the garden.	**present progressive**
3 She (to get) _____ up early.	**past simple**
4 She (to talk) _____ to me.	**past progressive**
5 She (to water) _____ her mango tree.	**present perfect**
6 She (to loll) _____ in the garden.	**past perfect**
7 He (to miss) _____ her very much.	**future**

Solving problems

> In many stories the characters face **problems** that the writer solves in one way or another.
>
> As a reader you may think the writer's **solution** is a good one, or you may feel you could have thought of a better solution.

1 Read the extract from the story on **pages 118 and 119** again. Make **notes** on an ending for the story in which you solve the problems that the characters have.

Does your ending:

- please the wife?
- please the young man?
- please the sister?
- please them all?

2 **Plan** and **write** a story in which the main character has one of the following problems:

- Your main character knows that his/her friend has broken the window in a neighbour's house.

  o Your friend has not told anyone what he/she has done.

  o What should your main character do?

- Your main character knows that his/her friend has borrowed a bicycle without permission and damaged it.

  o Although the friend is unhurt, the bike is badly damaged.

  o The friend has put the bicycle back and says nothing.

  o What should your main character do?

Travelling in India

Throughout our daily lives, we are surrounded by advertisements. They are on the television and radio, on posters, in newspapers and magazines, and on the Internet. Everywhere we look, there are words and pictures that are trying to persuade us to buy things, join things or visit places.

This is an advertisement on the Internet.

India will amaze you!

It's exciting, exotic and entertaining. India is a blaze of colour and a clamour of noise that will dazzle your senses. There are ancient ruins, fabulous palaces, bustling markets and tropical forests. India is a land of infinite variety. There are huge cities, peaceful villages, wild countryside and beautiful beaches. You can see the **Taj Mahal** at sunset, visit the **Amber Fort**, taste food as varied as the country itself and view some of the world's most beautiful wildlife. Come to India for your next holiday and you will be thrilled, fascinated and amazed. After your visit is over, you will want to return.

The Taj Mahal

Glossary

Taj Mahal a beautiful white marble building in Agra. It dates from 1623.

Amber Fort a palace near the city of Jaipur. It was built in 1592 from pale yellow and pink sandstone, and white marble.

You can use a dictionary to help you.

A Find each word in the advertisement. Choose the correct meaning.

1 exotic   **a** unusual   **b** boring

2 ancient   **a** modern   **b** very old

3 fabulous   **a** ordinary   **b** wonderful

4 bustling   **a** very busy   **b** empty

B Find these phrases in the advertisement. Discuss what they mean.

1 a blaze of colour   2 a clamour of noise

3 dazzle your senses   4 a land of infinite variety

Comprehension

A Discuss the answers to these questions.

1 What is the advertisement for?

2 What places can you visit in India?

3 What adjective is used to describe:

   a the forests?

   b the markets?

   c the villages?

B Write a sentence to answer each question.

1 Who do you think the advertisement is aimed at?

2 Do you think the advertisement gives a good description of India? Why? Why not?

3 Do you think this advertisement would persuade someone to visit India? Why? Why not?

C Find and copy three phrases that are used to persuade people to visit India.

This is an advertisement in a travel magazine.

Visit India for the holiday of a lifetime

Beaches so clean a turtle could eat its dinner off them. Seas as clear as glass, dotted with an occasional coconut that rolls in and out with the surf. Beaches of beautiful white sand that stretch for miles, edged by thickets of shady palm trees.

Word Check

You can use a dictionary to help you.

A Find each word in the advertisement. Choose the correct meaning.

1	dotted	**a** sprinked	**b**	covered
2	occasional	**a** very often	**b**	not very often
3	surf	**a** boat	**b**	waves
4	thickets	**a** a large group	**b**	a few

B Find these phrases in the advertisement. Discuss what they mean.

1 Seas as clear as glass   **2** stretch for miles

Comprehension

A Discuss the answers to these questions.

1 What particular part of India is being advertised?

2 What could eat its dinner off the beaches?

3 What occasionally rolls into the sea?

B Write a sentence to answer each question.

1 Who do you think the advertisement is aimed at?

2 Do you think the advertisement gives a good description of India? Why? Why not?

3 Do you think this advertisement would persuade someone to visit India? Why? Why not?

C Find and copy **three phrases** that are used to **persuade** people to visit India.

Similes

> A **simile** describes something by comparing it to something else.
> A simile almost always includes the words **as** or **like**.
>
> Seas <u>as</u> clear <u>as</u> glass
>
> The water sparkled <u>like</u> a jewel.
>
> You can use similes in your writing to create striking pictures with words.

A Choose the best word to complete each simile, or use a word of your own if you have thought of a better one.

1 as dry as a   field/desert/town/rock

2 as bright as the   moon/candle/sun/sky

3 as cold as   ice/water/fire/milk

B Write a sentence containing a simile about each of the following. Underline the simile in each sentence.

> Remember to use **like** or **as** in each simile.

1 a market

2 colourful fruit and vegetables

3 a palace

Punctuation

Commas in lists

> Remember, when we write **a list** in a sentence we use **commas**.
> We join the **last two things** in the list with **and**, **but** or **or**.
>
> This is the same when we are writing a list of **words** and when we are writing a list of **phrases**.
>
> There are ancient ruins, fabulous palaces, bustling markets **and** tropical forests.

A Copy the sentences. Add the missing **commas.**

1 We could go to the beach visit the Taj Mahal or visit the Amber Fort.

2 I'd like to go to a market a palace a village and the beach.

3 India has interesting cities peaceful villages wild countryside and beautiful wildlife.

4 He visited a busy market the beautiful Taj Mahal and a tropical forest but not the Amber Fort.

Spelling

ous, ious and **eous** word endings

> There are a range of words in English that use the suffix **ous, ious** or **eous**. For example:
>
> There are ancient ruins, **fabulous** palaces, bustling markets and tropical forests.

dangerous   curious   enormous furious jealous courageous
famous   previous generous serious various obvious

A Copy these sentences. Choose a word from the word box above to fill each gap.

1 Ashley saw an _____ elephant.

2 A _____ actor said how much he loved travelling in India.

3 We saw a snake but our guide told us it was not _____.

4 Mum was _____ when I accidentally spilt my drink.

5 Bedard was _____ when Verol won a huge chocolate bar.

B Choose three more words from the box. Write your own sentence for each one.

There are sometimes tricky letters in **ous** words. If there is an **i** sound (as in **fit**) before **ous**, the word usually has the ending **ious**. For example:

serious

If the word ends in **our**, we drop the **u** before adding the suffix **ous** or **ious**. For example:

humour   humorous

If a root word ends in **y** we drop the **y** and then add **ious**. For example:

fury   furious

C Add **ous** or **ious** to each of these words.

1 vigour   2 victory   3 glamour

4 vary   5 labour   6 harmony

Grammar

Fronted adverb clauses

Remember, to make sentences more interesting, we can use **adverb clauses**.

An adverb clause works just like an **adverb**. It tells us more about the verb.

An **adverb clause**:

> Adverb clauses are **subordinate clauses**. Subordinate means **less important**.

- has a **subject**
- has a **verb**
- begins with a **conjunction**, such as **because**, **when** and **if**
- answers questions such as **why** and **when**.

    Visit India **if you want the holiday of a lifetime**.

    adverb clause

Sometimes, an adverb clause can come **at the beginning of a sentence**. We put a **comma** after the adverb clause before the rest of the sentence.

    If you want the holiday of a lifetime, visit India.

    adverb clause

A Copy the sentences. Underline the adverb clause in each one.

1 He can travel around India when he has saved enough money.

2 He can travel around India if he saves enough money.

3 He can travel around India because he has saved enough money.

B Rewrite the sentences in **Activity A** so that the **adverb clause** comes **first**.

Remember the **comma**.

C Write **two** sentences using each adverb clause, so that:

- in Sentence 1, the adverb clause comes at the **end**.
- in Sentence 2, the adverb clause comes at the **beginning**.

The first one is done for you.

1 before we go to the market
We must have a meal before we go to the market.
Before we go to the market, we must have a meal.

2 after we visit the palace

3 unless we see an elephant

4 even though it is raining

Writing

Advertisements

Advertisements have to be attractive and eye-catching so you will take notice of them. People who design advertisements have to think about:

- **what the advertisement looks like**
  - **colour:** They may use bright colours, black and white, colours that go together or contrasting colours.
  - **layout:** This needs to be clear and easy to read, but also eye-catching and interesting. The name of what is being advertised and the title must be very noticeable.
- **illustration:** This could be artwork, photographs or diagrams.
- **what the advertisement says**
  - **persuasive language:** The advertisement needs to persuade people. The language used should say good things about what is being advertised.
  - **information:** The advertisement needs to give information about what is being advertised.

1 You are going to write an **advertisement for a magazine** about a **place you have visited**. This can be a place that you visited on holiday, a theme park, a museum or anywhere you like.

   a Plan your advertisement by making notes on the following points before you begin:

- the **place** being advertised
- **who** the advertisement is aimed at
- how you will make it **eye-catching**
- what **language** you will use to **persuade** people to visit.

   b Write the **first draft** of your advertisement. Think about:

- how you will **lay it out** on the page
- the **colours** you will use
- the **different sizes** of writing you will use.

2 Imagine you work in a travel agency selling trips to the Moon! Design an **advertisement** that will **persuade** people to go on the trip.

The Daily News

First Sri Lankan Climber to Reach Everest Summit!

by Rashmi Priyantha

At about 5 a.m. on 21st May 2016, Jayanthi Kuru-Utumpala became the first Sri Lankan person to stand on the highest peak in the world. With her climbing partner, Sri Lankan Johann Peiris, she left **Camp 4** to make an attempt on the summit. After some time, she continued on with her guide, Nepalese **Sherpa** Ang Karma and successfully scaled Mount Everest. At 8,848 metres, it is the highest peak in the **Himalayas**.

Jayanthi with her climbing partner Johann Peiris at Everest Base Camp

Jayanthi is a journalist and professional mountain climber. Her climbing partner, Johann, is a hair stylist. They teamed up in 2011. Together they have climbed Mount Imja Tse (also known as Island Peak) in the Himalayas, Mount Kilimanjaro in Tanzania, Mount Kinabalu in Malaysia and peaks in the **Andes** in South America. Before they climbed Everest, they trained hard. They spent two months in the Himalayas acclimatising before the climb. Both are known to be experienced and very determined, as well as mentally and physically tough.

Before the climb, Jayanthi said, "This will be our greatest challenge yet. At 8,848 metres above sea level, the legendary Mount Everest

Glossary

Camp 4 the last stopping place (camp) on the way to the top of Mount Everest situated at 8,000 metres

Sherpa a member of the Himalayan people who are known for their mountaineering skills

Himalayas a mountain range in Asia containing the world's tallest peaks

Andes a mountain range in South America

is one of the most testing physical challenges a human can attempt."

As the pair prepared to leave Camp 4, a colleague in their support team said that it was a strenuous overnight trek from Camp 4 to the summit. Johann Peries reached 8,400 metres.

Jayanthi on the summit of Everest

The climb above 8,000 metres is very dangerous and presents climbers with many challenges. The temperature is extremely low and there is only about a third of the oxygen found at sea level. This makes breathing and climbing extremely difficult.

Despite all the incredible difficulties, Jayanthi made it to the summit! She is the 419th woman to reach the top of Everest. In 1975, the Japanese mountain climber Junko Tabei was the first woman to achieve this feat. But Jayanthi has made it into the history books as the first person from Sri Lanka to stand on top of the world!

Word Check

You can use a dictionary to help you.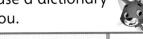

A Find each word in the article. Choose the correct meaning.

1 summit	**a** low ground	**b** top
2 scaled	**a** climbed	**b** photographed
3 acclimatising	**a** getting used to	**b** having fun
4 legendary	**a** little known	**b** very famous
5 strenuous	**a** needing a lot of effort	**b** needing little effort
6 feat	**a** something ordinary	**b** something extraordinary

B Find these phrases in the article. Discuss what they mean.
  1 mentally and physically tough
  2 made it into the history books

Comprehension

A Discuss the answers to these questions.

1 What is the newspaper report about?

2 When did Jayanthi reach the summit of Everest?

3 How high is Mount Everest?

4 Why are 'breathing and climbing' difficult above 8,000 metres?

5 Who is Junko Tabei?

B Write a sentence to answer each question.

1 Do you think the newspaper article has an eye-catching headline? Why? Why not?

2 Why do you think the reporter has included photographs?

3 How do you know that the reporter spoke to one of the support team?

4 Why do you think Jayanthi and Johann 'spent two months in the Himalayas' before they made the climb?

5 How do you know that the climb from Camp 4 to the top was done during the night?

C What is each **paragraph** about? Make notes.

Homophones

Homophones are two or more words that **sound the same** but have different spellings and meanings. For example:

They left Camp 4 to make **their** attempt on the summit.

There is only about a third of the oxygen found at sea level.

They're both known to be experienced and very determined.

The words **their**, **there** and **they're** are homophones.

A Write down each of the following words from the newspaper report. Next to each one write a matching homophone.

1 some   **2** our   **3** sea

4 to   **5** be   **6** peak

B Write four sentences, using a pair of homophones in each sentence. You can choose pairs of homophones from the box or use some of your own.

whether	to	here	hole	new
weather	too	hear	whole	knew

C Choose the correct homophones from the box to answer these clues.

stare	tail	flour	week
flower	way	weak	aloud
tale	allowed	weigh	stair

1 a part of an animal's body   **b** a story

2 a seven days   **b** not strong

3 a to measure how heavy   **b** the route you take

4 a part of a plant   **b** this is used by bakers

5 a something you climb   **b** to look for a long time

6 a the past tense of allow   **b** in a way that can be heard

Indirect speech

Direct speech is when we write the **actual words** that someone has spoken.

"Climbing Everest was Jayanthi's greatest challenge," he said.

Indirect speech is when we write **about** what someone has said.

- We **don't** use the exact words.
- We **don't** use speech marks.

For example:

He said that climbing Everest was Jayanthi's greatest challenge.

A Which of these is **direct speech**? Which is **indirect speech**?

1 "It's a strenuous overnight trek," said Jayanthi's colleague.

2 Jayanthis's colleague said it was a strenuous overnight trek.

3 The climber said that Mount Everest is 8,848 metres above sea level.

4 "Mount Everest is 8,848 metres above sea level," said the climber.

B Write each of these sentences using **indirect speech**.

1 "The temperature is very low above 8,000 metres," she said.

2 "Junko Tabei was the first woman to climb to the top of Everest," he told me.

C Write each of these sentences using **direct speech**.

1 The reporter said the support team was very helpful.

2 He said Jayanthi trained very hard for the climb.

Spelling

Words from French

The English language borrows many words from the French language. This section looks at three letter patterns the English language has borrowed from French:

ch (which sounds like **sh**)   para**ch**ute
que (which sounds like **k**)   anti**que**
gue (which sounds like **g**)   collea**gue**

For example:

As the pair prepared to leave Camp 4, a collea**gue** in their support team said that it was a strenuous overnight trek from Camp 4 to the summit.

The **gue** letter pattern, with a silent **u**, appears at the end of some words.

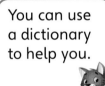

A Copy the words adding the missing **ch**, **que** or **gue** letter pattern.

1 ma___ine   2 catalo___   3 anti___

4 mousta___e   5 dialo___   6 ton___

7 uni___   8 para___ute   9 pictures___

You can use a dictionary to help you.

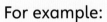

B Write down the answers to the following clues.

1 weariness   fa __ __gue
2 not clear   v__gue
3 people who work together   co__ __ __ __gue__
4 conversation   di__ __ __gue

C Use a dictionary to find the definitions of these words. Write down your answers.

1 catalogue   2 brochure   3 intrigue   4 unique

Grammar

Fronted adverb clauses

We can make sentences more interesting by using **adverb clauses** to add detail. An adverb clause tells us more about the **verb**.

Remember, an **adverb clause**:

- has a **subject**
- has a **verb**
- begins with a **conjunction**, such as **because**, **when** and **if**
- answers the questions such as **why** and **when**.

    For example:

    They trained hard **before they climbed Everest.**

    → adverb clause

An adverb clause can come **at the beginning of a sentence**.
We put a **comma** after the adverb clause before the rest of the sentence.

    Before they climbed Everest, they trained hard.

    adverb clause ←

A Copy the sentences. Underline the **adverb clause** in each one.

1 Many people have climbed Everest although it is very hard.

2 Climbing is more difficult when you reach 8,000 metres.

3 She must have felt wonderful after she reached the top!

B Rewrite the sentences in **Activity A** so that the **adverb clause** comes **first**.

Remember the **comma**.

C Write **two** sentences using each adverb clause, so that:

- in Sentence 1, the adverb clause comes at the **end**
- in Sentence 2, the adverb clause comes at the **beginning**.

1 when they left Camp 4

2 if we reach the top

3 before they left the camp

Newspaper reports

When you write a **newspaper report**, you should include these features:

- **a headline**   Make this as eye-catching as possible so readers will want to read the report.

- **byline**   This is the name of the person who wrote the report.

- **the facts**   Write about what actually happened. You can use dates and times, and place names.

- **background information**   You can tell your readers about events that led up to what you are reporting and include some background information about the people involved.

- **eye-witness accounts**   You can interview some of the people who saw or were part of what you are reporting.

- **illustration**   This can be a photograph, a map or a diagram.

1   Imagine you are a reporter at **one** of the following events. Make notes about the facts that you will include in your report.

- a New Year firework display

- an eruption of Mount Etna

- the Tacoma Narrows Bridge disaster.

> Looking back at these units will help you:
>
> Unit 6 *Let's Celebrate!*
> Unit 14 *Fire Beneath Our Feet*
> Unit 10 *Books About Bridges.*

2   Write a **newspaper report** about your chosen event.

- Think of an eye-catching headline.

- Make sure the reporter's name is on the report.

- Include the key facts about what happened.

- Add background information about the event and the people involved.

- Decide who you will interview and what questions you will ask.

- Think about how will you illustrate your report.

Check-up

Vocabulary

1 Write these words in **alphabetical** order: patch, pavement, peanut, past

2 Write the headings **Masculine words**, **Feminine words** and **Common words** and write each noun from the box under the correct heading.

> aunt   king   mum   child   doctor   queen   cat   uncle

3 Make a list of ten **synonyms** for **said**.

4 Write your own **definition** of these words, using only seven words.

   a birthday   **b** surprise   **c** gift   **d** friend

5 Write the **antonym** of each word.

   a happy   **b** dirty   **c** blunt   **d** strong   **e** polite

6 Write a **homophone** for each word.

   a bee   **b** there   **c** two   **d** weigh   **e** threw

7 Complete each **simile**.

   a as steady as _____   **b** as light as _____

Punctuation

1 Copy the sentences. Underline the **possessive noun** in each sentence.

   a My friend's party is on Saturday.   **b** The sailors' boat is safe.

2 Write these **singular** owners with an **apostrophe**.

   a the trees leaves   **b** the pirates treasure   **c** Jans call

3 Write these **plural** owners with an **apostrophe**.

   a the boys shoes   **b** the mens work   **c** the peoples rubbish

4 Copy the sentences. Underline the **plural noun**. Circle the **possessive noun**.

   a The volcano's eruptions went on for a long time.

   b The elephants' trunks are used for washing.

   c Have you seen the women's coats?

5 Copy the sentences. Add any missing **punctuation**.

    a I would like to visit that castle she said

    b Where are you going he asked

    c The wildfire is coming this way he shouted

6 Write these direct speech sentences as indirect speech.

    a "They learned about the Vikings today," said the teacher.

    b "The Vikings travelled in longboats," she explained.

    c "They travelled to America in their boats," she said.

7 Write these indirect speech sentences as **direct speech**.

    a His wife complained that she didn't help with the housework.

    b Her brother said that she looked after the tree.

    c His sister said that she should do more to help.

Spelling

1 Choose the suffix **able** or **ible** to complete each word.

    a favour_____   **b** terr_____   **c** comfort_____

2 Write an example word for each of these prefixes.

    a in   **b** auto   **c** ir   **d** dis

    e il   **f** super   **g** mis   **h** un

    i im   **j** anti   **k** re

3 Write the root word to which the suffix ending in **ion** has been added to make each word below.

    a expression   **b** observation   **c** rejection   **d** possession

4 Add the suffix **ly** to each word.

    a guilty   **b** simple   **c** angry   **d** critic

5 Write a **ure** word which rhymes with each of these.

    a treasure   **b** fixture

6 Complete these word sums.

    a glory + ous = _____   **b** nerve + ous = _____

7 Complete these words using **ch**, **que** or **gue**.

    a para ____ ute   **b** pla____   **c** ton____   **d** catalo____

Grammar

1 Write the **noun phrase** in each sentence.

    a That advertisement is very colourful.

    b The brave woman climbed Mount Everest.

    c Those people are visiting China.

    d The huge lion was sleeping.

2 Make each of these into a **noun phrase**.

    a _____ beach   **b** _____ tower

    c _____ bridge   **d** _____ rainbow

3 Add a **noun** to each adjective to make a **noun phrase**.

    a that huge _____   **b** an amazing _____

    c this violet _____   **d** the tallest _____

4 Write the **present perfect tense verb** in each sentence.

    a She has climbed the tallest mountain in the world.

    b He has visited lots of castles.

    c The birds have flown away.

5 Write the **past perfect tense verb** in each sentence.

    a She had watered the mango tree.

    b They had been to India before.

    c I had written a letter to my friend.

6 Write the **adverb clause** in each sentence.

    a The bridge collapsed after it was hit by a storm.

    b She completed the climb even though it was strenuous.

    c You won't see a rainbow unless it rains.

7 Write the sentences from the previous question so that the **adverb clause** comes first.

8 Copy and complete each sentence with your own **adverb clause** .

    a Smoke poured out of the volcano _____.

    b You should not go mountain climbing _____.

    c _____, I still want to go to the beach.